THE GDR

JENS SCHÖNE

THE GDR

A HISTORY OF THE "WORKERS' AND PEASANTS' STATE"

BERLIN STORY VERLAG

IMPRINT

Schöne, Jens:
The GDR—A history of the "Workers' and Peasants' State"
2nd edition—Berlin: Berlin Story Verlag 2015
ISBN 978-3-95723-020-1

Leuschnerdamm 7, 10999 Berlin
Tel.: (030) 20 91 17 80
Fax: (030) 69 20 04 059
www.BerlinStory-Verlag.de, E-Mail: Service@BerlinStory-Verlag.de
Translation: Simon Hodgson
Photo editing, cover and typesetting: Norman Bösch

WWW.BERLINSTORY-VERLAG.DE

TABLE OF CONTENTS

DEUTSCHE
DEMOKRATISCHE
REPUBLIK

PROLOGUE

THE GDR IN HINDSIGHT

East Berlin, 2 October 1988, evening. Thousands of people have made their way to the Werner-Seelenbinder-Halle in Prenzlauer Berg. The mood is cheerful and light-hearted. An event is about to take place here that, for a long time, has been considered impossible. Rio Reiser gives another concert just as he had the previous evening. The singer, from the neighbouring Federal Republic, enjoyed cult status. He had risen to fame in the 1970s with his band "Ton Steine Scherben". The band's songs touched a nerve with the people in the GDR. "Destroy what destroys you" or "no power for nobody" were cries that could be heard on both sides of the inner-German border. Reiser had been perusing a solo career for quite some time and had enjoyed considerable success. He was, as one of his hits referred to him, simply "the king of Germany".

He performed in the GDR. For a long time, those in power had tried to resist any sort of influence from the West. However, they felt increasingly compelled to offer more than the commonplace abundance of propaganda and state regulated rock music to the younger generation. This led the way to permission being granted for artists like Udo Lindenberg, Bob Dylan, Bruce Springsteen and other stars to perform in the "Workers' and Peasants' State". And now it was Rio Reiser's turn. He thrilled his audience and the concert hall was rocking. The concert was drawing to a close when the singer sang an old song by "Ton Steine Scherben": "Der Traum ist aus" (The Dream is Over). In the song, Reiser reflected on dreams he had once had, dreams which never

came true. The song then asks "Is there a country on this planet where dreams are reality?" and continues "I know one thing and I'm sure about it."

What happened next characterised the situation in the final years of the GDR better than any historical analysis ever could. The already extremely excited audience was beside itself with ecstasy, the level of sound exploded and thousands of voices joined to belt out "It's not this country, it's not this country!" There was no doubt about it, everyone there knew

^ *A saviour to the fans, a herald foreshadowing the end to the GDR: Rio Reise in East Berlin›s Seelenbinder-Halle.*

which country was meant with this chant: the GDR. Exactly two years later, the country would cease to exist.

But for now, it was not quite time. At this moment in time, there were very few signs that pointed towards the fundamental changes that were to take place in the near future. The Socialist Unity Party of Germany (SED) had ruled over the GDR for more than 40 years and it was not at all inclined to think that would change. There were reasons for this. The most important: the party considered itself to be on a historical mission which would lead humanity to a great future. Based on its Marxism–Leninism ideology, the party aspired to communism. There was no room for doubts. The SED considered itself the "vanguard" of the working classes. It was, in fact, avant-garde and assigned to the people a way forward without any alternative. It was with this plan that the SED came to power after the Second World War, a plan it would not give up on.

The German Democratic Republic (GDR) was a dictatorship. Contrary to what is sometimes claimed, this is not a retrospective description. Every East German child learned at school that the very best form of government existed in his country: the dictatorship of the proletariat. Children were taught that the dictatorship was to be defended against all enemies. From then on, during its ongoing battle against class struggle, this dictatorship would have to be established amid tough conflicts. Since the party, the SED, was never wrong, it would twist and turn a problem or negative development in such a way that made it look as though "enemies" of the people had caused it. Such people were to be dealt with firmly. This fundamental conviction that the party was always right led to any kind of digression from the official, predefined line becoming a punishable offence. The party defended its political position with all the methods seen in a dictatorship: human rights were disregarded, elections were rigged and both press and media were censored. Furthermore, the secret police threateningly watched over everything: the Ministry for State Security (Stasi).

Since the Peaceful Revolution in 1989/90, the mechanics of this dictatorship and how it came to power have been topics for many discussions and texts. Such discussions and texts were necessary and correct. That said, it is not so easy to explain why the GDR existed for over 40 years. The SED was not all-

powerful, the Ministry of State Security was not omnipresent and the country was not a giant prison in which everything was grey and sad. It would also not be appropriate to read the history of the GDR simply in the context of its downfall. The fact that it disappeared into thin air without so much as a whimper in 1990 does not justify the assumption that it had been heading towards this point from the very beginning.

So what, one has to ask, led to the self-proclaimed "Workers' and Peasants' State" becoming, in some respects, an integral part of the global community for four decades? How was it able to do this despite its opposition? How was it able to achieve periods of considerable success only for the people to then bring it down from power so dramatically? In other words: what prompted the citizens of the GDR to go along with the opportunism and repression that were part of the foundation and development of the state, or at least why did they accept this process without protest? When and why did the people finally lose interest and decide to choose a different path which ultimately led to the end of the GDR?

These questions form the backdrop for the following chapters. Following significant dates in the GDR's history, the founding, development, downfall and break-up of the country are all documented chronologically. At the same time, focus is placed on exactly what this process could have meant for the individual. Why he or she campaigned (or did not) and where stability existed that is necessary to preserve a political system over a long period of time. In order to answer these questions,

^ *Something that is often forgotten: everyday life exists even in a dictatorship. Snapshot taken on Prager Straße, Dresden in 1982.*

a different approach has been taken. The focus is neither on the Ministry of State Security, nor on the the opponents of the SED dictatorship. The Cold War between the superpowers, the German Question, bloc party politics and mass organisations are also less prominent focal points. Their significance for the GDR should, however, by no means be contested–that would be foolish. The book you are holding is, to a greater extent, the result of taking the aforementioned questions into account and the fact that these topics have been the focal points of intense research and conflicting opinions. There are many publications as a result, many libraries in fact. Anyone interested in information relating to these problems can look further into this with ease.

The GDR's coat of arms united hammer and sickle in a garland of corn. The intention was to make it symbolically clear exactly who prevailed in the state: above all workers and farmers–as allies to the intelligentsia. In reality, however, the supposed rulers (the workers and farmers) were subject to a well-orchestrated, one party dictatorship, and they would feel this. Particular attention is given to this fact throughout this book and for this reason there are many descriptions of events

^ *East Berlin, 1982: everyday life and dictatorship are interwoven. Anyone breaking with the norm can expect harsh consequences.*

that took place a long way away from those in power. A 53 year old cooling system in extremely poor condition, the problems it caused and how incompetent those responsible were in dealing with the matter, are highlighted. Focusing on such events reveals more about the overall condition of a society than theoretical discourse does. Those who believe that the events surrounding the Peaceful Revolution only took place in places like Berlin, Leipzig and Plauen have never heard of Großwudicke. Citizens there had already taken a stance long before the more well-known developments: "Now we're going to tear down the Wall." It is also necessary to tell their story.

"People are at the centre" this was a commonly used phrase in the GDR. To some extent, as already suggested, the same could be said for this book. For the first time and to the greatest extent possible, it is not only the big cities and their people that have been considered, but also smaller towns and communities throughout the country. The result is a range of new observations. Events around the people's uprising in June 1953 as well as the building of the Berlin Wall in August 1961 also appear in a new light. Furthermore, the question of what held the GDR together at its core can only be answered when one looks beyond the levels of government and instead at real-life situations. A further positive effect emerges from this: it becomes easier to explain why the events of 1989 appeared to happen so suddenly. The Peaceful Revolution was by no means the surprise it is often claimed to have been. Up until a few months before the end of the "Workers' and Peasants' State", stability, peace and order prevailed on the surface. It is, however, true that tensions had been bubbling for a long time, the system had become hollow and the people were no longer under any illusions. That was true beyond the cities–where it was said often and very openly. The dream was over. In this respect, Rio Reiser's performance was very symptomatic. Everything seemed to be business as usual, everything indicated that there would be "more of the same!" No change in sight, not anywhere. However, as would later be proved, a small prompt would be enough to achieve profound effects. "It's not this country" was an accurate description of the status quo and, at the same time, a prognosis for the future. We know what happened next.

^ *The GDR's regional structure since 1952: East Berlin as capital city and 14 districts which are also subdivided.*

ES LEBE
DIE NATIONALE FRONT
DES DEMOKRATISCHEN
DEUTSCHLAND

7 OCTOBER 1949
FOUNDATION OF A STATE

MOSCOW AND BERLIN

CONDITIONS

The future rulers arrived by plane and they had serious plans. Although, during the final stages of the war, nobody could say what the future held in store for Germany, some things were clear. The United States of America (USA), the Soviet Union, Great Britain and France–the most significant opponents to the German Reich–were already united by the general outlines of their occupation politics. The country was to be divided and each victorious power to assume responsibility for its own territory. This by no means meant that the future of the country was set in stone, especially not the emergence of two rival German states. It was, however, clear to those involved that fundamental changes were about to take place: "This war is not as in the past; whoever occupies a territory also imposes his own social system on it. ...It cannot be any other way."[1] With these words, Soviet head of state Joseph Stalin announced the Battle of Berlin in April 1945. The barbaric war, started six years earlier by the National Socialist dictatorship, had returned to its starting point. A short time later on 8 May 1945, the German army surrendered unconditionally, the military altercation in Europe was over and reconstruction had to begin.

There seemed to be a lot of possibilities against the backdrop of defeat, yet under Soviet hegemony, these possibilities were limited from the beginning. Stalin had not only thought about theoretical considerations in light of the pending occupa-

1 Milovan Djilas, Gespräche mit Stalin, Frankfurt/M. 1962, p. 146.

tion politics, but had also made practical preparations in order to bring forward his political system—the Communist dictatorship in the conquered territory. For the time being, such measures had to be carried out cautiously and covertly since the geopolitical interests of the Soviet Union went much further than the borders of their own occupation zone. Germany was just one of many things to be thought about in a worldwide game of power. Furthermore, the dictator was quite interested in collaboration with the Western powers at first, even if his real intentions were to ensure it would be possible to still have some sort of influence over their territories. To start with, direct confrontation should be avoided and changing the course should happen behind the scenes.

This being the case, a worker's group had formed in Moscow long before the end of the war and was made up of German immigrants who had fled there from Germany. It was their task to take what was deemed as necessary action after the Allied victory in order to implement the transformation process in the Soviet ambit. Members of this group were mainly old ideological Communists: Anton Ackermann, Wilhelm Pieck, Walter Ulbricht and many more. They had experienced the Stalinist terror in the 1930s, lost many comrades

^ *Wilhelm Keitel signs the unconditional surrender of the German army. Reorganising Europe could begin.*

without trace (and accepted this) and had absolutely no doubt about their mission: “We consider it the absolute best for our people, we would have a socialist Germany, a Soviet state.” The plans for post National Socialist dictatorship were not autonomous or even democratic, the plan was to apply the Soviet model–even if nobody said this publicly at the time. “The greatest flexibility in all tactical questions”[2] this was the dictate of the moment, but the aim of the politics had already been set: the “dictatorship of the proletariat”, the Communist dictatorship was to be established.

On the last day of April 1945, it was time. The first KPD (German Communist Party) officials set off for Berlin by plane from Moscow. Under Walter Ulbricht's leadership, they set up their quarters in Bruchmühle, not far from the German capital, and prepared themselves to carry out resolutions decided upon in Moscow. Their time had come.

2 Peter Erler/Horst Laude/Manfred Wilke (Ed.), "Nach Hitler kommen wir". Dokumente zur Programmatik der Moskauer KPD-Führung 1944/45 für Nachkriegsdeutschland, Berlin 1994, quotes p. 127, 170.

^ *Educated in Moscow and dispatched to the Soviet Occupation Zone with clear orders: Walter Ulbricht.*

"AND SO EVERYTHING IS IN THE BALANCE."

SETTING THE COURSE

The beginning was quite promising. The occupying forces installed the Soviet Military Administration in Germany (SMAD), which, from then on, was the highest authority in Soviet occupied Germany and, in consultation with Moscow, made all authoritative decisions. Almost immediately with its second order, the SMAD appeared to be levelling the way towards a diverse political future. On 10 June 1945, it came as a complete surprise when it was announced by the SMAD that parties would be invited to form in the Soviet occupied zone—much earlier than in any other occupied zone. Under the given circumstances, it was comprehendible that the SMAD reserved power to control and di-

Befehl Nr. 2

des Obersten Chefs der Sowjetischen Militärverwaltung.

Berlin, den 10. Juni 1945

Am 2. Mai d. J. wurde Berlin von den Sowjettruppen besetzt. Die Hitlerarmeen, die Berlin verteidigten, haben kapituliert und Deutschland hat nach einigen Tagen die bedingungslose Kapitulation unterschrieben. Am 5. Juni wurde im Namen der Regierungen der Union der Sozialistischen Sowjetrepubliken, der Vereinigten Staaten von Amerika, Großbritanniens und Frankreichs die Deklaration veröffentlicht über die Niederlage Deutschlands und die Uebernahme höchster Autorität auf dem gesamten Boden Deutschlands durch die Regierungen der angeführten Mächte. Mit der Besetzung Berlins durch die Sowjettruppen wurde in dem Gebiet der sowjetischen Besatzungszone Deutschlands eine strenge Ordnung hergestellt, wurden örtliche Selbstverwaltungsorgane gebildet und die notwendigen Bedingungen für eine freie öffentliche und politische Tätigkeit der deutschen Bevölkerung geschaffen.

Jn Anbetracht des oben Dargelegten befehle ich:

1. Auf dem Gebiet der sowjetischen Besatzungszone Deutschlands die Bildung und die Tätigkeit aller antifaschistischen Parteien zu erlauben, die sich das Ziel setzen, die Ueberreste des Faschismus mit der Wurzel auszurotten und die Grundlagen des Demokratismus und der bürgerlichen Freiheiten in Deutschland zu festigen und die Jnitiative und die eigene Tätigkeit breiter Volksmassen in dieser Richtung zu entwickeln.
2. Der werktätigen Bevölkerung der sowjetischen Besatzungszone Deutschlands das Recht der Vereinigung in freien Gewerkschaftsverbänden und Organisationen zu verleihen mit dem Ziel des Schutzes der Jnteressen und der Rechte der Werktätigen. Die Gewerkschaftsorganisationen und Vereinigungen zu berechtigen, Kollektivverträge mit den Unternehmern abzuschließen, sowie Versicherungskassen und andere Einrichtungen gegenseitiger Hilfe, kulturelle Aufklärungs- und andere Bildungseinrichtungen und Organisationen zu schaffen.
3. Alle in Punkt 1 und Punkt 2 angeführten Parteiorganisationen und freie Gewerkschaftsverbände müssen ihre Statuten und ihre Programme bei den Organen der örtlichen Selbstverwaltung, sowie bei den Militärkommandanten registrieren, indem sie gleichzeitig ihnen die Listen der Mitglieder der leitenden Organe vorlegen.
4. Zu verordnen, daß für die Zeit des Besatzungsregimes die Tätigkeit aller in Punkt 1 und Punkt 2 angeführten Organisationen unter Kontrolle der sowjetischen Militärverwaltung und entsprechend der von ihr gegebenen Jnstruktionen ausgeführt wird.
5. Entsprechend des oben Dargelegten die gesamte faschistische Gesetzgebung sowie alle faschistischen Verfügungen, Befehle, Verordnungen, Jnstruktionen usw., die sich auf die Tätigkeit der antifaschistischen politischen Parteien und freien Gewerkschaftsverbände beziehen und gegen die demokratischen Freiheiten, bürgerlichen Rechte und die Jnteressen des deutschen Volkes gerichtet sind, aufzuheben.

Der Oberste Chef der Sowjetischen Militärverwaltung
Marschall der Sowjetunion Shukow.

Der Stabschef der Sowjetischen Militärverwaltung
Generaloberst Kurassow.

^ *Approval of other parties gives an impression of pluralism; it was actually a step closer to dictatorship.*

rect; it was also comprehendible that the parties to be founded had to subscribe to anti-fascism and democracy.

As was to be expected, the members of the KPD trained in Moscow were first to rule, they had complete support from the Soviet side and were best prepared. However, the content of their founding manifesto from 11 June 1945 was astounding. It was those people in the population, who were still perceived as "servants" to the Russians, who also disassociated themselves from demands made earlier and the protecting powers. Their central committee emphasised that it was profoundly wrong to enforce a Soviet regime in Germany, there was a special, independent German way after all. Therefore, there would have to be concrete conditions initially to establish an anti fascist-democratic regime. At the same time, people's rights also had to be secured. The call offered a practical way to help master the challenges from the German side: by founding a "solid entity of democracy", a common block of all permitted parties. Grouping the powers like this also seemed sensible in summer 1945. However, it would become clear very quickly that an important device was needed to ultimately secure exclusive leadership for the KPD.

Four days later, the Social Democratic Party of Germany (SPD) raised its hand with its own founding proclamation which defined its standards for reconstruction and requirements for the future. The SPD also subscribed to anti-fascism and democracy, but in contrast to the Communists it clearly demanded socialistic elements in economy and society. Furthermore, the SPD stressed the need to unite the working classes as a result of what had happened during the turmoil of the Weimar Republic and the National Socialists' rise to power. This aspiration finally led to a consolidation between the SPD and the KDP. Respective demands were represented at the core of both parties. However, KPD leaders unequivocally rejected these aspirations in June. The KPD apparently feared it would be subdued by a much bigger party built on tradition if they were to merge into one.

Two further, more middle-class orientated parties completed the political spectrum in the Soviet Occupation Zone at first: The Christian Democratic Union (CDU) formed itself at the end of June, followed by the Liberal Democratic Party (LDP) at the end of July. Both parties were fundamentally for private ownership. The CDU, however, did not entirely rule out expropriation. And so, the CDU found itself to be in line with the KPD. However, it became clear during the course of the next year, that similar demands could be interpreted differently.

On 14 July 1945, the four parties created the anti fascist-democratic block—called for by the KPD—the unity front committee was supposed to serve as the coordinating top body and therefore speed up the implementation of commonly recognised basic demands. The parties formally agreed that all decisions made by the committee would have to be reached unanimously while acknowledging mutual recognition of independence. Furthermore, it was recommended that similar structures should be created at all levels, right down to the lowest administrative levels. What would later become known as 'democratic centralism' and would safeguard the power of the SED, had its roots here—even if that was hardly conceivable from the contemporary perspective. Politics could no longer be made against the KPD's veto. This applied also to all parties involved, but they were already lacking vital support: support from the Soviet Administration. It still appeared as though the parties were in an open competition, the first moves towards a dictatorship had, however, long since been made. Admittedly, it was not clear at first if these first moves would actually deliver the desired results.

Besides, in 1945—as was the case in all occupation zones—fundamental decisions were not made by Germany. It was the Allies of the Second World War who set the agenda, and under the difficult post war conditions they were also looking for quick and viable solutions to the various problems. At the same time, since the common opponents did not exist anymore, the conflicts of interest between the former allies were now coming to a head. In what was in many respects radically significant, a summit meeting was arranged and took place in Cecilienhof Palace in Potsdam from 17 June–2 August 1945. It was at this conference that the most important men from the Soviet Union, the USA and Great Britain met: Stalin (his only stay in Berlin), the American president Harry S. Truman and Winston Churchill (who lost the UK general election during the conference and was replaced by his successor Clem-

ent Attlee). Officially, the protagonists demonstrated unity, but that could neither hide the growing tension nor prevent the struggle behind the scenes. On the agenda at the 'Potsdam Conference' was still the fierce war in the Pacific, but above all the focus was on regulations which affected Europe. The regulations and agreements which formed 'The Potsdam Agreement'–the final report of the meeting–were comprehensive and were to have severe consequences. On the whole, agreements were reached that Germany should be denazified, demilitarised and democratised–as to what this meant in detail, no comprehensive statements were made. Sole territorial jurisdiction of the respective occupation zone was once more affirmed and, furthermore, it was established that this would serve as reparation for the war damages suffered. At the same time, this should also serve as a means of weakening Germany economically and preventing the country from becoming a future threat. Fundamental ramifications also led to agreements about forced resettlement of groups of the German population. This was to take place humanely but, in fact, resulted in mass chaos, suffering and misery.

Above all, the Potsdam Conference had shown one thing: indeed, it appeared that the former war Allies were still striving for unity, but in reality that had not been the case for a long time. Yes, the Allied Control Council had set up a committee which was supposed to deal with all high-level issues. How-

^ *Great struggles, fundamental decisions, and all very public: The Potsdam Conference in summer 1945.*

ever, for all practical purposes–with all due significance taken into account–it served only a minor role after a short time. On paper, Germany should be considered an economic entity, yet the extensive decisions by the respective occupying powers towards autonomy revealed that this intention had to be increasingly seen as a farce. The signs pointed towards growing antagonism between the Soviet Union and the Western powers; the signs were already pointing towards a world divided into two opposing spheres of interest.

The German population, in part, may well have been aware of this development, but it was not at the centre of their attention. The people, exhausted by war, had other, more pressing problems. The country had surrendered unconditionally, everyday life was hard and the future uncertain. The order of the state had decomposed, cities were in ruins, millions of men were in prisoner of war camps and at the same time, millions of displaced people were heading towards the zones of occupation. Any kind of infrastructure–electricity, water, transport, medical care–was stagnant and getting hold of food had become a daily struggle. The Russian zone of occupation still had a decent industry at the end of the war. It had been less affected by war damage than the Western zones and it appeared as

^ *It was the Allied Control Council's task to balance out the interests of the victorious powers. This quickly proved to be impossible.*

though it might be capable of post-war reconstruction. However, this fact meant little: the reparations, the large scale demolitions and the impoundments by the Red Army and the Soviet administration were a devastating blow for any potential the industry had. Some industrial sectors lost up to 80 percent of their capacity, 200 of the most significant businesses were converted to Soviet joint stock companies and produced only for the occupying power. Two years after the end of the war, half of the transport network was closed, and countless, in particular well-qualified and skilled employees were deported to the Soviet Union. These losses were almost too much, the Eastern zone of occupation was a society in collapse which had to find its feet once more.

Under such conditions, it was essential to kick-start the industry and agriculture. Shortly after the end of the war, the SMAD took steps to nationalise banks and other key industries, and the initiative was embraced by members of the KPD. Although it was by no means clear which were the necessary steps to take, the party leaders introduced a land reform at the beginning of September 1945. According to official statements, it was supposed to help with denazification and encourage distributional justice in small villages. There was general unity

^ *Public parks everywhere were converted into gardens in order to alleviate the desperate situation. Seen here, Tiergarten in Berlin.*

concerning the principle need for such a move, even agricultural experts had pushed for such measures in the past and the CDU supported them. However, the devil was in the detail. Central orders came directly from Moscow and the ruthlessness with which the Communist cadre acted horrified many people. All companies with a production area of more than 100 hectares were dispossessed without compensation–there were very few exceptions, church property being one. This was regardless of how valuable the space was, or whether or not the owner had shown resistance to the Third Reich. The owners were expelled from their ancestral homes and deportations took place once again. This is how one property owner and his colleagues from Saxony were deported to the island of Rügen. They were inhumanely deported in cargo trains and abandoned: "Please help us, please, [...] we're dying."[3]

These inhumane acts also had a reverse side. Large proportions of the expropriated land was shared out as smaller plots among poor, landless displaced persons. The plots had little chance of providing a long-term future, but secured short-term survival for their new owners and were for that reason welcomed, on the whole. And that was the actual purpose of the land reform: the KPD removed old elites out of the villages and created for themselves a clientèle with the socalled new farmers who secured their control in these areas. This was how the ideology was envisaged and this is also how it happened. Despite all the associated problems, the plan proved to be successful: 40 years later, the GDR people in the villages should look back thankfully at the benefits. The balance of power continued to shift, especially when the SMAD crushed the CDU leadership for speaking out against the SMAD's harsh actions and lack of compensation for the people.

Similar, superficial economically motivated measures affected the industrial sector. In spring 1946 and in close consultation with the Soviets, the KDP initiated the "referendum in Saxony". The result would lead to thousands of key industry operations being permanently expropriated. In this case, too, the propaganda whitewashed reality. The aim, according to the propaganda campaign, was the expropriation of war crimi-

3 Quoted in: Norman Naimark, Die Russen in Deutschland. Die sowjetische Besatzungszone 1945 bis 1949, Berlin 1997, p. 183.

nals and National Socialists. In fact, the party secured access to production and management: planned economy was looming. In June 1946, three quarters of those eligible to vote ultimately agreed on the referendum. And so, the desired precedent was created, the affected companies were nationalised and this model was then applied to the entire zone of occupation.

Just how serious the Communist Party was about seizing power–and the possibilities it had to do this–could be seen on an organisational level. As late as June 1946, the Communist Party had vehemently turned down a merge with the SPD, but now the party made a U-turn. There were very good reasons for this. By now, the KPD had been successful in gaining a dominant position among the other parties in the Soviet zone of occupation. However, the SPD remained the number one competition and outnumbered the KPD. Ideologically, social democracy was considered expendable since the KPD saw itself as the only legitimate representative of the working classes. Merging both parties under communist control would not only take power away from the most influential competitor, but would also sustainably strengthen the KPD's position. The occupying power clearly also realised this, applied massive amounts of pressure and eventually enforced organisational conformity. Despite a vote among Berlin SPD members yielding a rejection quota of 82 percent, the final steps could not be prevented in

^ *Gaining power by defamation: the KPD would go to any lengths to gain access to economical resources.*

Spring 1946: on 21/22 April, in East Berlin's Admiralspalast, the KPD and SPD united to become the Socialist Unity Party of Germany, the party that would control the fate of the GDR until its end.

The new party was flanked by a host of socalled mass organisations based on the Soviet model in which politics forced itself upon the entire social sphere, was led by communist cadre (who did not always announce themselves as such) and underpinned the united party from their side. The scale of these organisations ranged from the Free German Trade Union Federation (FDGB) to the Democratic Women's League of Germany (DFD), the Cultural Association of the GDR and the Free German Youth (FDJ). With the help of these institutions, every last individual should be accounted for and be committed to politics. By introducing these institutions, this goal was achieved in what appeared to be an apolitical manor. For this reason, scores more of these organisations were founded in the following years. It was not only in institutions that Communist cadre were able to give themselves important positions, members also took jobs in the judiciary and in the education sector, and modified these areas to better comply with their visions. This often took place under the pretext of the real need to denazify Germany (there were, however, no concrete criteria of how to go about doing this), but was all to often primarily a means of strengthening their own power. The principle for this was based on an internal directive given by Walter Ulbricht: "It has to look democratic, but we must have everything in our hands."[4] And this was how functionaries, as well as people who were deemed politically unreliable, were pushed out. This created room for new careers. They could, however, often only be pursued with SED approval. A few promotion prospects were being created, which until then had been unimaginable. Via these means, the party created support and its own loyal and faithful followers who would not only show support during its quest for political power, but in all sorts of crisis situations. Punishment and reward were ultimately two sides of the same coin and they would remain significant political instruments in the decades to come.

4 Wolfgang Leonhard, Die Revolution entlässt ihre Kinder, Cologne 1998, p. 440.

During 1946, the situation seemed to gradually stabilise and the post-war era to be coming to an end. However, the dark days of the past continued to have an effect and sometimes assumed new horrors. The ten socalled special camps built by the occupying power after the war embodied this. Officially, they served to hold active National Socialists and war criminals, but their purpose was quickly changing. The camps had been built partly on the sites of old National Socialist concentration camps, and increasing numbers of people who were against the emerging system (or better said, the Soviet administration) were imprisoned here. A simple slip of the tongue was sometimes enough for a sentence in one of these camps. Victims of denunciation were also put in prison as well as those who dared to address inhumane aspects within the regime (such as civilian rape by Red Army soldiers). The conditions in these camps were frightful: out of the more than 150,000 imprisoned, over 35 percent died. The suffering for those imprisoned did not end even after the dissolution of the camps. In the mid-1950s, many thousands were sentenced to long prison sentences in the notorious Waldheim trials. In the majority of cases, there was no defence, no witnesses and no hint of lawful justice—political justice was already very effective. It was forbidden to talk about this topic: the special camps, their history and consequences were complete taboo until the end of the GDR.

Consequently, the two years after the war were a time of great uncertainty. Nobody could say for certain how the future

^ *A symbolic gesture: Wilhelm Pieck and Otto Grotewohl shake hands in April 1946. The SED is formed.*

was to unfold. Diarist Victor Klemperer summed up the situation in an entry from mid-June 1945: "And so everything is in the balance."[5]

But under the surface, the initial foundations for the events ahead were laid. Very few people took this seriously, but in 1947 it would become clear that those in power were by no means interested in creating a democratic order. On the contrary. The cause for this was an international process which, in turn, had a drastic impact on the Soviet Occupation Zone.

5 Victor Klemperer, So sitze ich denn zwischen allen Stühlen. Tagebücher 1945-1949, Berlin 1999, vol. 1, p. 7.

HEADING TOWARDS TWO GERMAN STATES

At the end of the war, the USA had not made definitive plans about how it would get involved in Europe's future. It was still within the realms of possibility that US troops would pull out of Germany after the victory and gradually leave the continent. However, the more the former Allies distanced themselves from each other, the more tensions between them grew, and the chance that the American troops would leave became increasingly unlikely. From an American point of view, it was increasingly necessary to put a stop to a possible rise of Communism. A decision was made in 1947. The first indication of this was the Truman Doctrine. The political guidelines were released to the public in March by the President of America and promised all "free people" support while defending their right to self-govern. Three months later at the start of June, the Marshall Plan was drafted. This massive aid programme aimed to give a kick-start to the economy in a war damaged continent, create a close bond between

^ *In their zones of occupation, the Western Allies focus on economic development. Economic recovery was fast.*

providers and recipients and was aimed at all states—even those under Soviet control. By this point, the battle for European hegemony had really begun. The war had barely been over two years and a new one was already looming: the Cold War of the political systems. The political gap between the East and the West, which had existed a while already, was rapidly getting wider. For this reason, the *Communist Information Bureau* (short: Cominform) was founded in September 1947 under the leadership of the Communist Party of the Soviet Union (CPSU). At first, the SED was not permitted to join due to Stalin's view on a unified Germany. The aim was to coordinate the work of the Communist Party and comply with Soviet expectations. Along with this came the declaration of the Zhdanov Doctrine—a direct reaction to the Truman Doctrine and Marshall Plan. It said that the world had already split itself into two irreconcilable spheres of interest: an imperialistic, undemocratic half under US leadership and a democratic half under Soviet leadership. The breakdown was made final in December 1947 when a final attempt was made in London between the opposing foreign ministers to reach an agreement following which the Soviets left the Allied Control Council in March 1948. The bipolar world order was taking shape.

There was no way that this could continue without having some kind of impact on the inner developments of the Soviet zone of occupation. Indeed, the SED claimed to the protecting powers that its interests lay completely in a unified Germany, but this was just rhetoric. Behind the scenes, the course was being set for a permanent division of the two German states; even high-ranking members of the Soviet administration only talked about the matter internally. Since Stalin had still not given up hope of gaining access to areas and resources in the Western zones, this plan had to be kept quiet for the time being.

A full-scale reorganisation of the Soviet Occupation Zone ensued. In summer 1947, the Soviet Military Administration in Germany (SMAD) established the German Economic Commission (DWK), an administrative authority dominated by the SED. This regulatory instrument of power was set up to address all economical issues and would expand and eventually become a central part of the future GDR government. At

the same time, the SED was governing–this had been made easier by the expropriation that had taken place earlier–and was getting straight down to creating a controlled economy. An economy which should get rid of the uncertainties of the free economy, but which above all would secure party access to resources, people and operations. It was now no longer hidden that the process was about much more than economic issues. While discussing initial plans, Ulbricht left no doubt it was the job of the SED as "a socialist party" to lead the way in the "solution to the collectivity of the democratic, economic and organisational task."[6] This was nothing less than a claim to absolute power. Anyone who was opposed to this claim or anyone who protested it would have to reckon with consequences. The CDU had found this out in December 1947 when its leaders were deposed from the SMAD for exactly these reasons.

In order to restructure the SBZ in favour of the SED and to take potential votes away from the centre-right parties, the occupation force founded two new bloc parties in spring 1948: the Democratic Farmers' Party of Germany (DBP) and the National Democratic Party of Germany (East Germany) (NDPD). While it was the task of the first to penetrate rural areas, it

6 Der Wirtschaftsplan für 1948 und der Zweijahrplan 1949/50 zur Wiederherstellung und Entwicklung der Friedenswirtschaft in der sowjetischen Besatzungszone Deutschlands. Referent: Walter Ulbricht, in: Thomas Friedrich/Christa Hübner/Herbert Mayer (Ed.), Entscheidungen der SED 1948. Aus den Stenographischen Mitschriften der 10. bis 15. Tagung des Parteivorstandes der SED, Berlin 1995, p. 125.

^ *The SED enforced massive changes even in villages. The continual land reforms until 1948 were the starting point.*

was the task of the latter to recruit those who had once been members of the Wehrmacht or Nazi party. By law, the process of denazification had been declared as over at the start of the year, but former followers were to be integrated as tightly as possible into the new political line.

It was the SED itself, however, that was to undergo the most significant change. Led by KPD officials, who had been trained in Moscow, the party was transformed to a "Partei neuen Typus" (new kind of party). If, at least officially, it had until now been based on the same model from the time of its foundation–Communism with social democratic elements–this was now over. The party was remodelled against the backdrop of the close connection to the international Communist movement, it was radically committed to the ideology of Marxism-Leninism and subject to the principles of "democratic centralism". That meant strict hierarchies, on paper it meant votes for all functionaries, but in reality it meant strict adherence to the party. Members now had to follow their leaders unconditionally, and dissenting opinions were not tolerated any longer. A special parliamentary control commission was set up and kept a watchful and inquisitive eye on the unity and purity of the party. Untrustworthy members–or those deemed to be–were cleared out at irregular intervals. Under Josip Brots, Yugoslavian communists had refused to follow the Soviet Union in June 1948, that was not to happen again in Stalin's dictatorship. It was for this reason that the transformation into a "new kind of party" took place in almost the entire Eastern block and also the reason why the Soviet dictator went a step further. He revoked the theories of special, national paths to socialism and declared his own to be universally valid. Deviation from this was no longer possible.

This development did not cause any discontent among the leaders of the former KDP who had been trained in Moscow. Quite the opposite in fact, they were ideologically fixated on the Moscow model and instead of considering the Stalinisation of their party and the entire sphere of influence as patronising, they viewed it as progress. It seemed as though the time had finally come to realise its extensive claim to power. The confrontation between the victorious powers of the Second World War was coming to a head and had created a climate in which

it became possible, in domestic politics, to rigorously enforce their own ideas, to transform economy and society and get rid of power rivals. There were growing indications in West Germany that there was going to be an independent state. America and Britain had already joined forces in January 1947 to form the Bizone, where further steps were being openly discussed. All signs were pointing towards the formation of an independent state in the East in the near future. An independent state which would consequently be led by the SED, even if it was merely borrowing it from the Soviet Union.

However, things were to turn out differently one last time and it would be a result of international conflicts. In mid-June 1948, the Western powers announced that a currency reform was to take place and that the Deutschmark would become the only legal tender in their area of influence. By introducing a single currency in the Western zones, the two German economic zones became even more alienated from each other. This was deemed unacceptable by the Soviet side and it also introduced a currency reform a few days later, one that had already been in the planning for some time. There was a more telling reaction from the Soviet side in response to the currency reform in the West. Berlin was the location for these events, the city had also

^ *The currency reform was a cause for concern in the Western zones of occupation, but it quickly proved to be a success.*

TÄGLICHE RUNDSCHAU

Zeitung für Politik, Wirtschaft und Kultur

Demokratische Währungsreform in der sowjetischen Besatzungszone und in Berlin

Interessen des werktätigen Volkes berücksichtigt / Ein Beispiel sozialer Gerechtigkeit / Weitgehende Möglichkeiten für Entfaltung der Industrie und Landwirtschaft geschaffen

BEFEHL

des Obersten Chefs der Sowjetischen Militärverwaltung in Deutschland Nr. 111

Inhalt: Ueber die Durchführung der Währungsreform in der sowjetischen Besatzungszone Deutschlands

been divided into four zones of occupation–they were called sectors. Soviet troops blocked off the Western sectors and the first Berlin crisis unfolded. The aim of the move was painfully obvious: ideally the Western powers would be forced to withdraw, leaving the rest of the city to be integrated into the Soviet sphere of control. What happened, however, was very different. With the aid of a giant airlift, the Western powers flew in essential supplies to the city and in doing so won over massive amounts of popularity with the people.

They thwarted Stalin's attempts to gain power over the Western sectors, and the Western powers slowly turned from occupiers into friends. For the Soviets, in contrast, the blockade was a disaster and in May 1945 it was abandoned.

Whenever it was in conflict with Western opponents, and the focus was on gaining more territory if nothing else, the SED could hardly hope to be allowed to form its own state which would thereby make other accomplishments possible. This was made painfully clear to the SED when it was called to Moscow in December 1948. What Stalin himself announced there was a wake up call to the SED. Instead of talk-

^ *The Soviets announced their own currency reform for their zone in June 1948, then they blocked off West Berlin.*

ing about hopes for a state foundation, the dictator suddenly talked about altogether different matters. He compared the the actions by SED leaders up until then–which should not have been able to happen without his permission–with the actions of "Teutons". Their "battle" had been "too open", they were not once "on the brink of power". He did not even allow it to be proclaimed that his occupation zone was a people's democracy. In terms of propaganda, that would have been the next step towards socialism, but for now it was not to happen. It was revealed once again that Stalin's interests were not only in the East German Communists. The Soviet zone of occupation was indeed an important part of his sphere of influence–but clearly just one part of many.

^ *The Western Allies sent supplies to West Berlin via air (above), children reenact it eagerly (left).*

Nevertheless, there was hope for Wilhelm Pieck, Walter Ulbricht and the accompanying comrades. Per se, Stalin did not doubt the main aim in the Soviet zone of Occupation. He did, however, order "opportunist policies towards socialism", "not direct interventions, but indirect."[7] However, it should not take ten months, playing tactically was over.

7 Rolf Badstübner/Wilfried Loth (Ed.), Wilhelm Pieck – Aufzeichnungen zur Deutschandpolitik 1945-1953, Berlin 1994, quotes p. 260pp.

^ *Waiting, and queues of people are part of everyday life. Seen here in East Berlin during the currency reform.*

THE FOUNDING OF THE GDR

7 October was a Friday, it was a fine day in autumn. It was a day that would go down in history. The People's Council met in the afternoon in the German Economic Commission building (the former Air Ministry building), not far from the sector border to West Berlin. Founded and directed by the SED, it announced itself as the provisional government and its constitution was put into force. And so, the German Democratic Republic, GDR for short, was born. Wilhelm Pieck became president, Otto Grotewhol the first prime minister and East Berlin became the capital city.

Likely staged events were seen: hundreds of thousands of members of the Free German Youth movement gathered on Berlin's boulevard, Unter den Linden, and paid homage

^ *Wilhelm Pieck, first and only GDR president, talks about the foundation of the country. Moscow listens closely.*

to the new state and its leaders. The fact that there was also a torchlight procession, which was all too reminiscent of the last dictatorship, did not seem to cause alarm. Pledging his oath to the GDR was a comparatively young SED official, Erich Honecker. People would hear a lot more of Honecker in the future. Cheers rang out: to the GDR, its representatives and obliviously to the supposed best friend to humanity, Stalin.

Always doing things in style at the time, Stalin returned the compliment two days later with a gushing telegram in which, among other things, he wrote the following:

> "The formation of the peace-loving German Democratic Republic is a turning point in the history of Europe... If you lay down the foundation stone for a unified, democratic and peace-loving Germany, you are accomplishing a great achievement for all of Europe."[8]

There seemed to be a contradiction here: the foundation of a separate state as the basis for a unified Germany? Indeed, the coming years would prove that Stalin meant that seriously. To him, the GDR was a model which should be expanded and applied across all of Germany. Not to mention that it would have also meant an expansion of his sphere of power. Hereafter, his East German governors would have to keep emphasising that they were "protectors of German unity"–although in reality

8 Neues Deutschland, SED party newspaper, 15 October 1949, p. 1.

^ *East Berlin, Unter den Linden, 11 October 1949. Public celebrations surrounding the foundation of the "Workers' and Peasants' State".*

they were doing everything in their power to block off their country from the West. The contradiction between propaganda and reality could not have been greater.

The founding of the state was by no means a surprise. After the altercations surrounding the Berlin Blockade had been argued out, the aforementioned constraints no longer applied. Furthermore, Basic Law (German constitution) had already been announced as valid in the Western zones of occupation on 23 May 1949. On 7 September, the Bundestag and Bundesrat were formed in Bonn after free and democratic elections–the Federal Republic of Germany saw the light of day for the first time. Stalin, who had seen this coming and waited patiently, then went on to allow the formation of another state. This one, however, had been called for by officials in Moscow; there was no talk of an election. The GDR was a child of the Cold War, but also of the Soviet Union's forcefulness and the SED cadres' hunger for power.

In keeping with the framework set by the occupying powers, the SED had spent the previous years paving the way for building up the 'dictatorship of the proletariat', which in reality was going to be the dictatorship of its party. Talk of a socialist GDR was still unofficial at this point, but the way towards it had been marked out. Vast transformations had already taken place in the towns and villages of the newly founded state that had ousted old elites and created new careers. The bloc parties and mass organisations had been brought into line; there was going to be no resistance. Setting up the People's Police, po-

^ *West Germany is also born in 1949. On 23 May, German Law (Grundgesetz) is announced (centre: Konrad Adenauer).*

litical lawsuits, arbitrary verdicts and blaring propaganda were part of the bigger picture already; any resistance against the set course was crushed forcefully.

The fact the SED, which by this time already had over two million members, could make its way to power so quickly had its reasons; reasons that went beyond opportunism, repression and Soviet support. Its worker party myths offered the proletarian milieu the chance to belong to something. Furthermore, it presented itself as a radical alternative to the National Socialist regime. In this respect its core message was not to be ignored: nobody else was turning away from the sinister past so resolutely while working so resolutely on the future at the same time.

The fact that it was evidently exploring altogether different options did not change anything in terms of the anti-fascist pathos to which it held on to, and which secured supporters (and maintained them) until 1989. If nothing else, the idea of a politically left state had long enjoyed a certain following–including and above all among intellectuals.

This idea now seemed as though it was becoming reality. But this was also a myth and those who believed it was becoming a reality were fooling themselves. There were plenty of these people.The GDR lacked legitimisation from its own people and at no point in its future would the government be democratically elected.

^ *In accordance with central directives, events throughout the GDR celebrate its foundation, here in Dresden on 12 October 1949.*

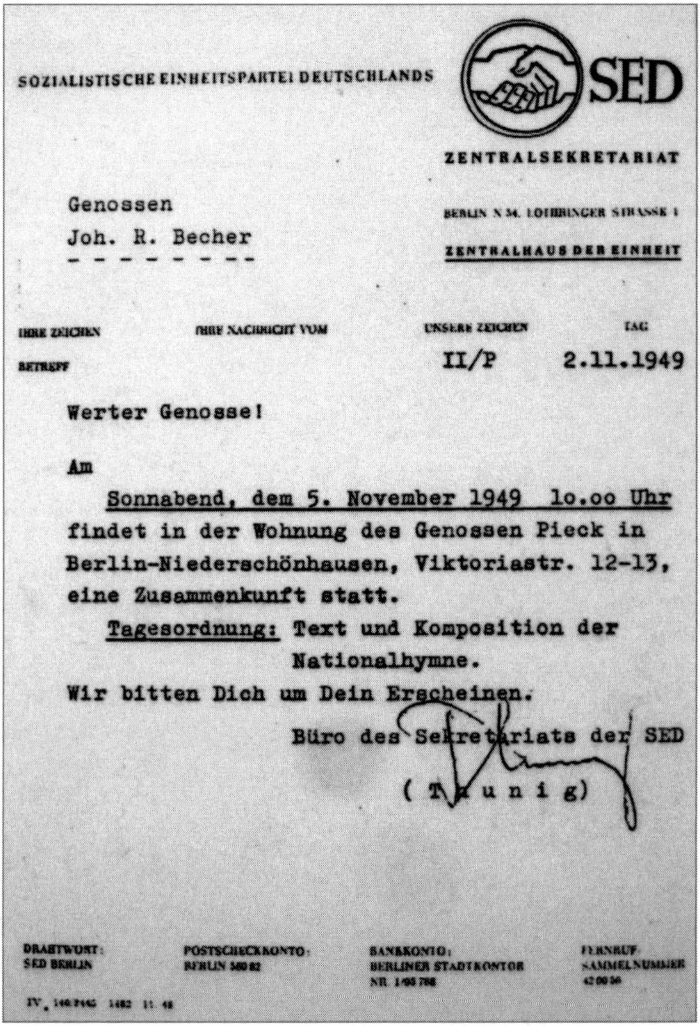

SOZIALISTISCHE EINHEITSPARTEI DEUTSCHLANDS

SED

ZENTRALSEKRETARIAT

BERLIN N 54, LOTHRINGER STRASSE 1

ZENTRALHAUS DER EINHEIT

Genossen
Joh. R. Becher

IHRE ZEICHEN | IHRE NACHRICHT VOM | UNSERE ZEICHEN II/P | TAG 2.11.1949

BETREFF

Werter Genosse!

Am
Sonnabend, dem 5. November 1949 10.00 Uhr
findet in der Wohnung des Genossen Pieck in Berlin-Niederschönhausen, Viktoriastr. 12-13, eine Zusammenkunft statt.

Tagesordnung: Text und Komposition der Nationalhymne.

Wir bitten Dich um Dein Erscheinen.

Büro des Sekretariats der SED

(Tunig)

DRAHTWORT: SED BERLIN | POSTSCHECKKONTO: BERLIN [illegible] | BANKKONTO: BERLINER STADTKONTOR NR. [illegible] | FERNRUF: SAMMELNUMMER [illegible]

^ *Another symbol of national pride is in the making: the national anthem. Its text was only sung until 1972.*

Nur eine gesamtd
überwindet die

^ *East Berlin 7 October 1949. Foundation of the German Democratic Repbulic by the SED-led people's council.*

17 JUNE 1953
UPRISING AGAINST THE DICTATORSHIP

CLAIM TO ABSOLUTE POWER

In wake of the foundation of the GDR, the Soviet Military Occupation in Germany (SMAD) handed over its administrative functions to the provisional GDR government on 10 October 1949. The SMAD had now become the Soviet Control Commission (SKK) and formally it only served to ensure that Allied rulings were adhered to. In effect, the SKK ultimately remained the most influential authority; as and when required, and after consultation with Moscow, it alone passed necessary resolutions and could intervene in the actions of the SED leaders. On the surface, Moscow let its East German comrades act as they wished–and they knew how to use this to their advantage. The extent to which the party was already on its way to setting up a monopoly became clear just a week later. An internal ruling had been made, a ruling which was valid throughout the GDR's entire history, a ruling which only came to light after the Peaceful Revolution in 1989/90. It revealed the true power structure within the "Workers' and Peasants' State". It was not the people, not the parliament, nor was it the government that controlled the fate of the country, it was the SED party and the SED party alone. The directions given on 17 October 1949 are clear:

> "Before being passed, laws and regulations of importance, any other materials used in passing government decisions, and proposals for enactments of laws and regulations must be conveyed to the People's Parlia-

ment, the Politburo or the Politburo's secretariat for resolution."[9]

9 Matthias Judt (Ed.), DDR-Geschichte in Dokumenten. Beschlüsse, Berichte, interne Materialien und Alltagszeugnisse, Bonn 1998, p. 77.

"Conveyed for resolution" meant that from then on, no fundamental decisions would be made unless they were made by the leading members of the SED or the Politburo, or at least not without their approval. The SED was borrowing its power

^ *Those in power continue to demonstrate massive presence, like here during a large-scale raid on Alexanderplatz in Berlin.*

from the Soviet Union and it had long since marginalised its domestic competition. The block parties and mass organisations now only served to give a sense of pluralism to what was actually autocracy, and to help incorporate as many GDR citizens as possible into the establishment. There was no hint of a democracy; the SED now had all the decisional power.

In order to secure and expand its dominant position, the SED quickly took a number of steps which coincided with its Stalinist, cadre party politics and would shape the future of the GDR. After the war, with the agrarian reform (Bodenreform) and the 1946 referendum in Saxony, radical changes in land

ownership structures had begun. This led to the deployment of one the Communist movement's tools, a tool that had already proved itself over the last few decades in the Soviet Union and was already being tried out in other Eastern European states: the show trial. The industrial sector, agricultural co-operative banks–there were show trials against all sorts of bodies. Throughout the country, these public spectacles of propaganda aimed to crush traditional, independent structures and replace them with new, ideologically defined structures. Cleaning up and bringing the judicial system into line made the process easier. The trials were officially justified with feigned reasons. It was claimed the trials were being held to expose and show the "henchmen of the fascist rulers" and that there could be "no leniency for enemies of our peaceful developments"[10]. Anyone who was not willing to integrate unconditionally into the predetermined SED way of life had to reckon with persecution and long prison sentences. At the same time, the party also secured access to employment vacancies and production, this put it in a better position to be able to offer further jobs to its supporters.

However, it was not only alleged SED enemies who felt the brunt of its lust for power and transformation–even its own members were increasingly under scrutiny. The party had been undergoing cleansing since the late 1940s. In 1951, it seemed like this cleansing was about to reach its first peak. Undesirable, and above all differential comrades were removed from the party with the help of "self-criticism". Those

10 Landes-Zeitung. SED newspaper for Mecklenburg, 10 July 1951, p. 1.

who came under suspicion for not following the party line were at risk of losing their party membership, career chances, prestige and, in many cases, their jobs. The party gave and the party took: more than 150, 000 members were cast out in 1951. The silver lining to these measures was the enhanced sense of discipline and pressure to adapt that was felt by the remaining party members. The idea behind this was summed up in the "Lied der Partei" (Song of the Party) which was always aggressively recited. It not only glorified the SED as "mother of the masses", but also simply declared "the Party, the Party is always right". Opposition to this was not tolerated, no matter where it came from.

At the start of the 1950s, the SED announced the foundation of its organisation which would help to expand its totalitarian claim to power against any opposition. The organisation would become synonymous with spying, repression and tyranny: The Ministry for State Security (MfS). Secret police had already existed in the Soviet Occupation Zone/DDR–the infamous "K 5" criminal investigation department was similar–but it was not until the MfS was founded on 8 February 1950 that this type of structure was institutionalised concretely. Primarily set up with few personnel and, therefore, not very much power, it was developed to become one of the most important tools for the SED in its quest to hold onto power. There was never any question surrounding the chain of

^ *One of the first large show trials took place in Dessau in 1950. Leo Herwegen, former minister, was also on trial.*

GESETZBLATT

der

Deutschen Demokratischen Republik

1950	Berlin, den 21. Februar 1950	Nr. 15

Gesetz über die Bildung eines Ministeriums für Staatssicherheit.

Vom 8. Februar 1950

§ 1

Die bisher dem Ministerium des Innern unterstellte Hauptverwaltung zum Schutze der Volkswirtschaft wird zu einem selbständigen Ministerium für Staatssicherheit umgebildet. Das Gesetz vom 7. Oktober 1949 über die Provisorische Regierung der Deutschen Demokratischen Republik (GBl. S. 2) wird entsprechend geändert.

§ 2

Dieses Gesetz tritt mit seiner Verkündung in Kraft.
Berlin, den 8. Februar 1950

Das vorstehende, vom Präsidenten der Provisorischen Volkskammer unter dem 10. Februar 1950 ausgefertigte Gesetz wird hiermit verkündet.
Berlin, den 18. Februar 1950

Der Präsident
der Deutschen Demokratischen Republik
W. Pieck

command: the SED alone could give orders and they were followed unconditionally and without question by the MfS which was the SED's "sword and shield". This would be the case for almost 40 years.

^ *Two paragraphs with far-reaching consequences: the foundation of the Stasi was officially made public at the end of February 1950.*

INTENSIFIED CLASS STRUGGLE

THE FIRST ATTEMPT AT SOCIALISM

In just a few years, and to a bewildering extent, the SED had managed to become the sole centre of power in the GDR, it had silenced its competition and gained control of society and the economy. Things were indeed moving forward in the torn country. At the start of the 1950s, the post-war era was over, a fragile daily routine was taking hold and the standard of life appeared to be improving. It was possible to believe that the future was bright if one pretended not to see the dictatorial actions of the SED, and instead listened to and believed the announcements it made. Many believed that the party would not be able to keep up its methods of transformation in the long-term.

That, however, was a fatal mistake. The massive changes over the last few years were not the end, they were just the beginning. Those in power were still concealing their real aim: to build up a socialist state following the Soviet's example. This step was still refused for the time being due to the Soviet Union's foreign policy. The Soviet Union was still hoping to extend its control over all of Germany and prevent West Germany from integrating with Western alliances. One last attempt to achieve this was made in spring 1952. In early March, the Soviet Union passed on the socalled Stalin-Note to its former allies. The note outlined negotiations towards a German reunification. Under its terms, Moscow would decide how reunification was to take place. For this reason, the terms were completely unacceptable to the Allies and they refused them outright. Stalin's all-German ambitions faded and the path for

implementing his own political system in the GDR was free. As a result, the SED leaders were called to Moscow in early April and given lessons in the change of policy. Once again, it was made clear: despite all of its dominance within the GDR, the SED remained a Russian puppet, had no power when it came to fundamental matters, and was merely a body to implement authority. To the German comrades, however, that was not a flaw. The Soviets were still the sole instigators of the communist movement and were to be followed unconditionally. On its return from Moscow, the SED administration implemented the first instructions given to them. The borders to West Germany (but not to West Berlin) were closed off. They began setting up an army and dissolved the existing federal states, replacing them with 15 boroughs as part of a structural reform. The ultimate and massive change in course followed

^ *Blocking off the inner-German border followed from May 1952. Here, part of the border between Thuringia and Hesse.*

two weeks later at the second SED party conference where Walter Ulbricht, the SED's general secretary, announced:

> "The political and economical conditions, as well as the consciousness of the working class and the majority of those in work are so well developed that setting up socialism has become the fundamental task in the German Democratic Republic."

He went on, and the following is of particular significance: "It should be noted that the intensification of the class struggle is unavoidable and the workers must break the resistance from the enemy forces."[11] When referring to the "workers", he actually meant the party and was formulating a declaration of war—a declaration of war which would lead to the People's Uprising of June 1953.

What followed was a year of relentless, unbridled exercise of power by the SED. Based on theoretical Marxist-Leninist writings and the Soviet Union's example, the SED took the leap toward forcing socialism on the GDR. In the frenzy of the class struggle, the party lost any kind of standards and oppressed almost every level of society. Cordoning off the inner-German

11 Dokumente der Sozialistischen Einheitspartei Deutschlands. Beschlüsse und Erklärungen des Zentralkomitees sowie seines Politbüros und seines Sekretariats, Ed. by SED Central Committee, vol. IV, Berlin (East) 1954, p. 73.

^ *A central landmark in the GDR's history. The SED decides to set up a socialist state during its second party conference.*

border had torn apart families, contact and traditions. Remilitarisation bound finances and resources and meant the consumer was deprived. The expansion of heavy industry, ordered by Stalin, was felt negatively in almost every other area. All of this cost money, money the SED state had to get from somewhere. There were no lengths the SED would not go to in order to get this money. Retailers, tradespeople, farmers and other self-employed citizens were subject to tax and duties at previously unheard of levels. Those who were not able to pay were stripped of property, punished and locked up. Long-term imprisonment was a real threat–even for the most minor offence–and sentences were much harsher than they had previously been. It is important to consider exactly who was being tried: these individuals were not enemies nor capitalists, but the people. Any boiler

^ *Socialism should also be adhered to in the villages. The SED sent industrial workers to crush resistance.*

man who took his own coal home with him, any baker who gave away unsold bread, any woman taking from harvested fields–they were all sentenced to long-term prison sentences. Between July 1952 and May 1953 alone, the number of people in prison rose from 31,000 to more than 66,000. The people were to be educated and converted to socialist utopia, and the government would go to any lengths to achieve this. The situation was aggravated by expropriation of the most sickening kind. Based on one single decree, more then 6,500 farms were nationalised in just six weeks at the start of 1953. Only a few weeks later, more than 600 hotels and restaurants were seized on the Baltic coast as part of "Aktion Rose"; an entire section of the hospitality sector disappeared almost overnight.

A further, more aggressive process of transformation which saw more conflict and further consequences affected rural GDR: collective farming. The aim was to put an end to private farming and replace it with a network of state controlled agricultural cooperatives (LPG). Private farmers were to join "voluntarily", but very few wanted to do so. Merciless force was deployed. Officials close to the SED in such communities were given weapons, farmers were vilified, show trials were organised and much more. If protest was shown, it was suppressed with a vengeance. The "intensified class struggle" had now reached the GDR's villages. No consideration was taken for traditions, established structures or local knowledge. It was necessary to adjust life to fit in with ideology. As far as the SED was concerned, collateral

^ *The role model for socialism and intensifying class struggle was obvious: the Soviet Union.*

damage was unavoidable. This meant that the entire population's food supplies deteriorated drastically.

At the same time, those in power were fighting on many more fronts: middle class remnants were removed, campaigns against the church (in particular against "young members") were introduced, not even the individuals who ran the state—the workers—escaped: socio-political achievements were revoked, prices were raised, certain foods were withdrawn and work loads were increased. All of these measures could be traced back to the SED's thirst for power and its vision of a happy, socialist future. It had neither sought the approval of its people, nor had it ever legitimised its control. By now, the party was waging a war on its own society. The "intensified class struggle" was to enforce what the majority obviously did not want. Then, suddenly and with no further explanation, the SED fundamentally changed its policy once again.

^ *Class war meant victims throughout the country, like here in Wismar. The "Reuterhaus" hotel was dispossessed.*

Junge Welt — Extrablatt

ORGAN DES ZENTRALRATS DER FREIEN DEUTSCHEN JUGEND

Sonderausgabe | April 1953 | Preis 10 Pf.

Aus dem Inhalt:

Tatsachen über Jugendmißhandlungen in den Pfeifferschen Stiftungen Seite 3

Ein Sturm des Protestes gegen das Treiben der „Jungen Gemeinde" Seite 4

„Junge Gemeinde"-Tarnorganisation für Kriegshetze, Sabotage und Spionage im USA-Auftrag

Schändlicher Mißbrauch des christlichen Glaubens / „Junge Gemeinde" wird von den westdeutschen und amerikanischen Imperialisten dirigiert / Enthüllungen über die Verbindungsleute der „Jungen Gemeinde" im Westen / Ehemaliger Gestapo-Agent – als „Diakon" getarnter USA-Spion

Die Korrespondenten der „Jungen Welt" aus allen Teilen der Deutschen Demokratischen Republik berichten über neue Tatsachen der feindlichen Umtriebe der illegalen „Jungen Gemeinde". Diese Tatsachen, die wir uns verpflichtet fühlen der Öffentlichkeit zu unterbreiten, runden das bisher durch zahlreiche Beiträge der „Jungen Welt" gezeichnete Bild dieser illegalen Organisation ab. Es erweist sich, daß die heuchlerisch mit christlichem Schein verbrämte „Junge Gemeinde" direkt durch die in Westdeutschland und vorwiegend in Westberlin stationierten amerikanischen Agenten- und Spionagezentralen angeleitet wird. Der christliche Glaube vieler junger Menschen wird durch eine geschickt aufgebaute religiöse Staffage mißbraucht, um sie unter Vorspiegelung angeblich kirchlicher Betätigung nicht nur gegen die Deutsche Demokratische Republik aufzuhetzen, sondern auch zu feindlichen Handlungen, die schweren Strafen unterliegen, aufzuwiegeln. Somit ist die „Junge Gemeinde" nichts weiter als ein verlängerter Arm der Terrororganisation BDJ. Ihre Leiter sind die gleichen, die in Westdeutschland im Auftrage Adenauers und seiner amerikanischen Hintermänner eine Hetzjagd gegen die für Frieden und Einheit mutig kämpfende Jugend veranstalten und solche aufrechten jungen Patrioten wie Jupp Angenforth verhaften, verschleppen und mißhandeln. Die Hintermänner und Leiter der „Jungen Gemeinde" wollen — wie die Tatsachen beweisen — in unserer Republik ein gleiches System des Terrors aufrichten wie in Westdeutschland, sie besorgen die schmutzige Sache Adenauers, des Todfeindes der deutschen Jugend.

Das sind die Hetztafeln der illegalen „Jungen Gemeinde"

Ein angeblicher Studentenpfarrer

Greifen wir zunächst etwas zurück.

^ *Repression and redevelopment at the same time. "Youth Congregations" made headlines for being enemies, and Stalinallee in Berlin quickly took shape.*

THE PEOPLE'S UPRISING

On 9 June 1953, the SED Politburo made an announcement which would go down in history as "The New Course". It was published a few days later and above all, it was one thing: a political declaration of bankruptcy. For the first (and last) time, the party, which claimed it was always right, admitted to making a mistake. The array of actions to be taken profoundly counteracted the reckless behaviour of the last few months. Almost every development which had been pushed for since the 2nd party conference was to be reversed, and old methods were to be implemented again. Private companies, it was announced, would be reopened, forced tax was to be suspended, price increases and cuts in social benefits were to be withdrawn, the campaign against the "Junge Gemeinde" (Youth Congregation) should be ended, farmers would be given back their rights, and much more. More particularly, all court rulings made in accordance with the "intensified class struggle" were to be reassessed and all prisoners who had served up to three years were to be released immediately. A change of course could not have been more drastic; failure could not have been more clearly documented.

Had the SED-leaders recognised that their social war against their own people had not brought about the desired results and decided therefore upon a change in course? Far from it. If it had have been up to Walter Ulbricht, Wilhelm Pieck and other prominent SED comrades, nothing, absolutely nothing would have changed so quickly. Fundamental decisions were still not being made in Berlin, but in Moscow. And in Mos-

cow, things had changed with one crucial event: Stalin had died on 5 March 1953. His potential successors fought bitterly for his power, but aspired to consolidate the entire territory. With regards to the GDR especially, this seemed highly advisable. Admittedly, the Soviet top-ranking officials were not surveying the situation in the GDR in great detail, but there was one thing that greatly unsettled them. As a result of the failed politics since summer 1952, the number of people turning their backs on the GDR and seeking happiness in West Germany had dramatically increased. In March 1953 alone, it was 31,000 people. The number of people fleeing from rural communities had increased by an astonishing 1000 percent within a year. In terms of propaganda alone, that was nothing short of a catastrophe and in Moscow it was considered as an increasingly real threat to the existence of the East German federate state. Moscow was convinced that the country could not afford such another blow. In June 1953, the SED leaders were called back to the Soviet capital and the next move was enforced on them.

^ *A funeral procession makes its way along Stalinallee on 9 March 1953. The Soviet dictator is buried in Moscow on the same day.*

This move would be seen in the "New Course". The aim was to stabilise the situation, but exactly the opposite happened. The people, who had experienced the class struggle firsthand in the last few months, and who had been punished harshly by the state for the smallest of mistakes, demanded changes in the party, most significantly Ulbricht's resignation. This, however, was not to happen. Furthermore, a crucial aspect of the "New Course" was not brought forward: fair pay for workers. It had been announced at the end of May that all work quotas were to be raised by up to 10 percent by 30 June–Ulbricht's birthday. That could effectively lead to wage cuts of 20-40 percent since, more often than not, bonuses could not be paid for exceeding targets. The working class, who, according to the official doctrine, ruled the country, was seething.

Before the storm broke out in the cities, it was the villages that revolted. This took place nationwide and even today it is not a well-known fact. It was, however, in the small communities where the rebellion began. Immediately after the "New Course" was announced, there were official reports of victory celebrations in every region; the end of the SED's control and the upcoming reunification of the two German states were celebrated. Collective farming had affected villages everywhere harshly and it is not hard to understand why countermovements were seen throughout the country. Exactly how explosive the mood was, and how volatile the actions taken in

^ *According to the government, the increase in labour standards came about voluntarily and were celebrated, like here in Leipzig on 1 May 1953.*

the villages were, became clear by 13 June. A place of particular significance was Körner in Thuringia. It was here that a meeting (actually to do with harvesting) was held. Things escalated. Chants of "out with the mayor"[12] were cried, and the chants quickly turned into death threats. Advancing police prevented a murderous end to the confrontation, but on the same evening, local representatives–with the exception of SED members–decided to recall the mayor from office. This was a highly political, unthinkable act until then, and similar scenes were being played out at this time in other villages.

Before 17 June 1953, there was public resistance in several GDR towns and cities. On 12 June in Brandenburg an der Havel, furious citizens demonstrated and attacked public buildings. In the district of Meißen, workers went on strike against increased work quotas. And in Güstrow, on 16 June, workers at a midsize company protested publicly against the imprisonment of their junior director. The GDR was in uproar, but the nationwide fuse was yet to be lit in order to spark a national People's Uprising.

On 16 June 1953, in the afternoon, it was time. After a few disturbances the previous day, a protest march gradually formed along the construction sites on Stalinallee in East Berlin. The march was initially protesting against the increased

12 Announcement by telephone on 13 June 1953, in: Jürgen Gruhle, Ohne Gott und Sonnenschein. Eine Dokumentation, vol 3, Nauendorf 2002, p. 39.

^ *In Jessen (district of Cottbus), farmers from neighbouring villages gathered and enforced the release of their colleagues.*

work quotas. However, it did not stop there. Further demands were quickly made. The situation escalated in front of the House of the Ministries, in which the GDR had officially been formed in 1949. Despite the announcement at around 2:30pm that the labour standard had been revoked, the demonstrators did not disperse. On the contrary, they made demands for free and democratic elections which would have meant an end to the SED dictatorship. They also called for a national strike to take place the following day. Free press from West Berlin had been reporting the events throughout the day. When the workers slowly scattered into the night, everyone involved waited anxiously to see what would happen the next day.

In many regards, 17 June brought clarity. The next day, people allover the country revolted. By now, it was not just about increased work quotas or cuts to social benefits. It was now a question of power. The demonstrators' demands everywhere were alike; not because there was any kind of central control to the uprising, but because the uprising was a reaction to the "intensified class struggle" of the past months. This was the starting point for the same problems that were causing the same resentment and the same demands. As was already the case in the villages, towns and cities nationwide now demanded an end to SED rule and a reunification of the two German states. More then 700 places in the GDR took

^ *Berlin became the focal point for the uprisings, the demand to lower labour standards is just one of many.*

part in the uprising, more than one million took up an active stance on the streets. Berlin remained the most visible centre, but similar scenes were seen right across the country. There was widespread calm in the morning. The rebels were confident and considered themselves victors. They sang anti-socialist songs, attacked government representatives and chanted their demands. The end of the SED regime seemed close. The people's refusal was all too apparent.

But then, Red Army troops intervened. It had been decided in Moscow overnight that any sort of rebellion would be suppressed using all available means. A breakaway by the Soviet's Western outpost had to be prevented. This was particularly important, as if it was not prevented, it could lead to more freedom movements in other countries. It was necessary to make an example of the GDR. In accordance with this decision, armed forces moved in. Wherever it seemed necessary, brutal measures were taken, and, in some cases, protestors were shot. For the most part, however, the troops' presence, their abundance of military vehicles and their threatening orders to break up the protests were sufficient. Just a few years after the war, very few dared to take on what had become the victorious power.

A state of emergency was announced in more than 167 of the 217 GDR districts, while the East German party and gov-

^ *Citizens in Leipzig's inner-city also protest and attack the prison and state security buildings.*

^ *At Potsdamer Platz, the border between East and West Berlin, the situation escalates at noon on 17 June.*

ernment leaders watched from the sidelines at the Red Army's headquarters in Karlshorst, Berlin. Meanwhile, it was apparent that the uprising lacked clear demands in order to achieve success. There was no clear and definite aim. It lacked a leader, as well as logistics and communication, considerable preparations had not been made. The uprising had spontaneously taken place at short notice and was resolutely suppressed. It did, however, make way for a few further protests. In some towns, protests did not begin until 18 June and there was unrest in the villages until the end of the year. Principally, however, its fate had already been sealed on the evening of 17 June 1953. It was over and it had cost at least 55 people their lives.

^ *Like here in Berlin, Soviet tanks were seen in great numbers throughout the GDR. They helped break up the uprising.*

^ *Berlin, scenes of the People's Uprising. The red flag is pulled down from the Brandenburg Gate, the black-red-gold flag is hoisted.*

^ *The demonstrators take their anger out on objects and buildings that represent the system.*

^ *The tanks start to roll around noon. Senior occupation zone representatives try to calm the situation. This fails miserably.*

^ *The demonstrators are still convinced they will succeed, they voice their frustration clearly. However, the situation changes.*

^ *Dismay spreads. The demonstrators try to get to West Berlin over the inner-city sector border.*

^ *It is impossible to stand up to a Soviet tank. The streets begin to empty, the people vanish.*

^ *By evening, the situation is under control. West Berlin is cordoned off. Such massive protests would not be seen again until 1989.*

13 AUGUST 1961
WALLED UP UTOPIA

CALM AFTER THE STORM

The People's Uprising deeply shocked the rulers and, until 1989, it remained the biggest trauma for the SED leaders. However, neither a noteworthy analysis of the cause was ever carried out, nor was there a significant change to the party line. On the contrary, already in mid-June 1953, any doubt disappeared: party leaders announced that the "general line was and remains right"[13]. Party propaganda quickly claimed that the events had been a fascist putsch, it referred to it as "Tag X" (D-Day) and claimed it had been caused and driven by West German spies in order to sabotage the GDR's success. Despite great efforts, not even the Stasi could prove this. It did, however, remain the official account of events until the end of the GDR. The government could create as many legends as it wanted, but nothing could change the fact of the matter. 17 June had quite clearly shown that the self-proclaimed party of the working class did not command the majority, and its survival was only thanks to Soviet troops. Should that support ever crumble, the government's power would be subject to negotiation.

For the time being, however, it was necessary to stabilise the GDR and pacify a country in uproar. This became increasingly possible by using the carrot and stick approach. Up to 15,000 people were arrested for their involvement in the People's Uprising, most of them were set free by the end of the year. At the same time, more then 1,500 were sentenced to

13 Central Committee resolution from 26 July 1953, in: Dokumente der SED, vol. IV, p. 467.

long-term prison sentences by German courts by the end of 1954. Two very questionable death sentences were also passed. Once again, there were countless show trials. With the help of the show trials, the SED aimed to prove that it was not its politics that had caused the revolt, but counter-revolutionary acts carried out and controlled by enemies of the working class. Not even its own ranks were safe from the bout of punishment being handed out. The party was being cleansed again, and not even high-ranking officials escaped unscathed. Article 14 of the GDR's constitution stipulated that "The union's right to strike is warranted". Justice Secretary Max Fechner made a public reminder about this and paid for doing so with an eight year sentence of hard labour. Soviet military tribunals sentenced up to 750 of those who had taken part in the uprising. Ironically, they were to be lucky under the circumstances: in 1955, when the Federal Chancellor Adenauer reached agreements for the return of German prisoners of war from the Soviet Union, those sentenced for involvement in the uprisings were also included. In contrast, those sentenced by German courts mostly had to sit their entire sentence.

As well as criminal persecution, which aimed to have an overt and deterring effect, the SED expanded its surveillance and repressive apparatus. The Stasi, which for the time being was downgraded to the State Secretariat for its failure in the run up to the uprisings, underwent a massive structural and staffing expansion. The People's Police, represented locally by community policeman (ABV) until then, was gradually extended to become a comprehensive network. The mass organisations were orientated more greatly towards the surveillance of the people, and the Combat Groups of the Working Class were rigorously increased; a general, radical militarisation of the system and of society would not go unnoticed.

But that was only one side of the coin. Alongside its repression, the SED was looking for a way to compensate the stricken people. It (for the time being) renounced the "intensified class struggle" very publicly and also implemented the previously announced "New Course". Private ownership was given more importance, the campaigns against the church weakened and collective farming was no longer forced. Labour standards were reduced and social benefits vouchsafed. The party and

the Ministry for Justice reviewed political judgements dating back to the time before the uprising, and within a few months they released around 24,000 prisoners. It seemed that an altogether moderate period was dawning and that a period of de-Stalinisation was underway: the press was suddenly reserved, there was more freedom for expression in art and culture than before and even the perpetual propaganda seen in the previous months broke off. There was suddenly talk of freedom and pleasure, even the consumer market improved noticeably. The SED appeared to be concentrating on cooperation with the people as opposed to confrontation. To put it simply, the party had indeed learnt from its failed politics of class struggle: if the party was to act too harshly, it risked society rising up against it again. For the time being, that was to be avoided at all costs, stabilising the situation was the priority for now. This had nothing to do with having an insight into its own mistakes, nor with a fundamental change in policy, even less so to do with tolerance. As would soon be shown, safeguarding power was the main priority.

^ *Combat Groups of the Working Class during the 1 May demonstrations in 1954. The Combat Groups have been undergoing expansion for a few months.*

FROM DE-STALINISATION AND BACK AGAIN

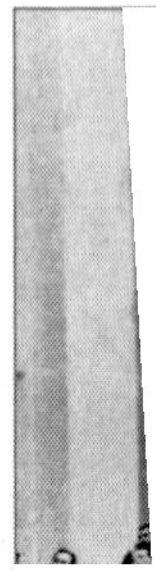

In the wake of the People's Uprising, the situation throughout the Eastern block calmed down. The Soviet hegemonic power allowed the state more freedom than ever before. It did not, however, at any point forego its claim to leadership.

In 1955, the Soviet Union even formally granted the GDR complete sovereignty, the presence of hundreds of thousands of Red Army soldiers, however, ensured its hegemony. In reality, the SED carried on taking orders from Moscow.

Just as those in power in East Germany were recovering from recent events, and their territory had been pacified, there was another blow. This blow, however, came from a completely different and altogether unexpected place. In February 1956, the 20th Congress of the Communist Party of the Soviet Union was held in the Russian capital. The party's first secretary, Nikita Khrushchev, made a "secret speech" in which he was suddenly very critical of his predecessor, Stalin. Khrushchev claimed that Stalin had massively abused his power and promoted a cult of personality. He had ordered the annihilation of whole populations, had become a megalomaniac and been responsible for countless more mistakes. Such talk had been unimaginable until then and the SED members present must have been absolutely astounded to hear it. After all, they were Stalin's most fervent students and, despite their changes in course since 1953, they had never doubted his person or his politics. In the GDR, Stalin was still considered to be one of the most significant communist figures. Pictures of him hung in public buildings, Stalin monuments lined the streets and

the cult personality created by Khrushchev—which he himself had paid homage to for a long time—was part of every day life.

Exactly what had been said in the "secret speech" spread quickly in the Western media and the SED had to react. Walter Ulbricht did just that on 4 March 1956 in the official SED newspaper "Neues Deutchland". His words immediately became legendary: "Stalin cannot be considered a classic Marxist". At best, that was a halfhearted dissociation and for good reason. Nobody else in the history of the GDR had influenced the top-ranking officials quite as Stalin had and that was still evident. The shock of the People's Uprising was still apparent. An abrupt change of East German state policy given from Moscow had almost caused collapse. Repeating such events was to be avoided.

It would not have been wrong for Ulbricht to consider his hesitant actions as being correct. Elsewhere, the process of de-Staliniation began and neither Moscow nor East Berlin wanted it. While there were pockets of regional protest against the communist dictatorship in Poland, which were quickly brought under control, a massive People's Uprising in Hungary eased off. As had been the case in the GDR three years earlier, the protesters here were also demanding independence for their state, and basic rights for themselves. Once again, the reaction from the Soviet side was quick and drastic: Red Army troops quelled the uprising alongside Hungarian communists with a great deal of bloodshed. The old order was restored and little was to change until 1989.

^ *The Communist Party of the Soviet Union's 20th party conference. The new strongman at the lectern: Nikita Khrushchev. German delegate Ulbricht on the right.*

The double U-turn from decreed de-Stalinization and brutal suppression of all actual reform movements was not without consequence for the GDR. Unrest spread in two areas; unrest which the SED leadership warily faced straight away. Any kind of deviation from the official line could spiral out of control and have unexpected consequences, this had been proved in Hungary. It was, therefore, necessary to act. Rural universities, which were considered rebellious, were the first to encounter this action. Strict guidelines were issued by the SED which now made it possible to suppress even the smallest protest, to expel university students and to exclude unruly lecturers from teaching. Quite rightly, the party and Ministry of State Security sensed an "anti-Soviet mood" and a "hostile stance towards the SED, the state and its leading functionaries." A public statement made by a forestry student at the Humboldt University shows just how volatile the atmosphere was. This also represented how many others felt:

> The student "accuses W. Ulbricht of pursuing a cult of personality und claims that W. Ulbricht is not the most suitable comrade for the job of 1st Secretary, and that he was not voted in democratically (...). He is of the opinion that the party will therefore never be able to win the trust of the masses."[14]

The question of power had been raised. It was at this point that an end to leniency was seen, and any deviants were punished with draconian methods. Philosopher and SED member, Wolfgang Harich, for example, suffered harshly. In the heated atmosphere of 1956/57, he had called for modest changes, but had by no means criticised the SED dictatorship. That, how-

14 Request for disciplinary action from 15 March 1957, in: Humboldt Universität zu Berlin, University Archive, stock: Forstwirtschaftliche Fakultät in Eberswalde, file reference: 241.

^ *Wherever the threat of resistance stirred, it was crushed, like in Hungary in 1956.*

ever, was enough, and an example was to be made of him. Harich was sentenced to ten years hard labour, and many of his colleagues also received similar sentences. The message this sent out was aimed at all intellectuals in the GDR and ultimately at the entire population: whoever contests the existing conditions in the reputed "Workers' and Peasants' State" had to fear the retribution of the party. The years of limited liberalism were over, a process of re-Stalinisation began, orthodoxy and dogmatism took charge again.

The change in course was even felt by SED comrades. A new wave of cleansing swept through the unsettled party to align it with the valid party line and remove the fickle members. Countless full-time officials lost their positions and a massive struggle for power among the top-ranking officials was calmed down. Even those involved in the power struggle were only interested in minor changes and not in a fundamental shift in politics. Nevertheless, the battle was fought out hard and ultimately settled by signals from Moscow. In Moscow, any kind of change was being avoided after the events in Hungary. This kept the power in Ulbricht's hands, and kept it out of reach from his opponents, the most prominent being Politburo member, Karl Schirdewan and Minister of State Security, Ernst Wollweber. Both of these opponents had lost their positions at the top due to "factionalism".

The controversies within the SED and at the universities initially had little effect on the people of the GDR. People kept a close eye on what was going on, but were not directly impacted. People continued to leave the country for the West, but even these numbers were falling slightly. The economic miracle that was slowly beginning to take shape in West Germany passed the GDR by, where important foodstuffs were still

^ *Wolfgang Harich became a symbol of attempts at reform. He felt all too well the GDR's inability to reform*

rationed. Things were, however, slowly moving upwards. The SED had toned down its rigid exercise of power, the same could be said of the tiring propaganda campaigns. These factors made life in the GDR seem more bearable and hope for the future was great. Then came 1958.

^ *Economically, things were indeed on the way up. Self-service shops were the newest trend, hope for the future was great.*

A NEW ATTEMPT AT SOCIALISM

Socialism is the aim of all politics (later on, Communism), the top-ranking East German officials, at least, had never doubted this. The first attempt had completely failed in 1952/53. However, after the intra-party conflicts had been fought out, it seemed like the time had come to try again. The assumption that socialism would soon enjoy global triumph was a crucial contribution to this belief. There were also indications that this would come true, the most important of which was in outer space. In October 1957, the Soviet Union sent the first artificial satellite into space. This was the trigger for the dramatic "Sputnik crisis" which broke out in the entire Western Hemisphere. It was feared that the USSR would close the technological gap between itself and the USA, and then go on to win the Cold War. Furthermore, the communist country's gross national income had shown a steady increase of more then 10 percent. It seemed only a matter of time before capitalism would be beaten once and for all. As far as progress was concerned, optimism knew almost no boundaries on the socialist side of the Wall.

There were even signs in the GDR that the positive trend from the previous year would continue. The subsistence level rose, the first Trabant (East German car) left the factory in Zwickau in 1957, the last food coupons were abolished in 1958, and cultural life was brighter than ever. Things looked good. This bound important sections of society tighter than before to the existing conditions and thereby also to the SED. This bond, however, was fragile. The fact that the people refrained from any extensive resistance (there were, however, definitely

individual cases), certainly did not mean that they shared the party's aims. The SED did still consider itself to be on a historical mission. Driven by controlling optimism of progress, once again the party drastically changed its course in mid-1958. It was time to implement what had failed so miserably in 1953. The logic behind it demanded above all one thing: all structures, bodies and mindsets that deviated from the pure teachings of Marxism-Leninism had to be fought with every last bit of energy and, when in doubt, suppressed. This is how real socialism was to be forced upon the people, a socialism that would prove superior, and to which the future belonged to. The extent to which the top-ranking officials were convinced of this line of action was revealed at the fifth SED Party Conference. It was at this conference in July 1958 that the "Main Economic Task" was defined specifically. Its success took priority above everything else. Its aim was

> "developing the national economy within just a few years to such an extent that the superiority of the socialist social order over capitalism is proved. For this reason, the consumption of vital provisions and consumer goods per capita among the working people must be higher than it is in West Germany."[15]

15 Resolution made at the fifth Party Conference, in: Dokumente der SED, Berlin (East) 1961, vol. VII, p. 259.

^ *The Trabant went into production in Zwickau in 1958 and would become part of the face (and smell) of the GDR until its end.*

The hopeful plan, which quickly gained fame with its slogan "Überholen ohne einzuholen" (overtake without catching up), also showed the SED's main weakness: West Germany was still a positive model for large proportions of its own people, the other German state was still depicted as being more economically successful and offered a democratic alternative to the GDR. For these reasons, countless numbers of people continued to leave the self-proclaimed "Workers' and Peasants' State". It was necessary to create a setting that would change all that.

The initial steps towards this had already been taken. The Ministry of State Security had reacquired its status, and Erich Mielke became minister after the intra-party disputes. In the same year, a cultural conference set up by the government lashed out at the decadence of Western art and claimed that the only possible form of expression was "social realism." Police, the judicial system and the apparatus of the state were all subjected to a further process of consolidation. Once again, dissenting opinions were considered grounds for exclusion from many possible career paths. Anyone who levelled criticism had to pay with negative consequences in their life. This was particularly harsh for one section of society who, until then, comparatively, had managed to hold on to their autonomy to a greater extent: the farmers.

After the initial wave of collectivisation, a widespread sense of calm set in. The storm, however, took hold again. The rea-

^ *Highest visit from Moscow. Nikita Khrushchev personally approved the decisions made at the fifth SED party Congress in July 1958.*

sons were the same as they had been in 1952/53. The SED regarded the rural population as retrogressive. At the same time, there were autonomous agricultural businesses throughout the GDR. While this had not been the case in the industrial sector for a long time, resources in the agricultural sector were predominantly privately owned, and that was a great source of frustration to the SED. Moreover, these farmers in rural areas were almost completely evading both the planned economy and Marxist-Leninist ideology. Under the mantle of constructing a socialist state and as part of the "main economical task", this would not endure–the party began a major coup to take over the villages. After a preliminary phase, the "Socialist Spring" began in 1960. From the very beginning, its aim was to crush all privately run rural businesses and to force their produce and their owners into Landwirtschaftliche Produktionsgenossenschaft (LPG) (Agricultural Production Cooperatives), which would then be controlled by the state and party. It was a success, and within just three months, many hundreds of thousands of villagers, who had until then refused such a move, joined the LPG. The reasons everywhere for this were the same: troops were spread out through the GDR and by using forceful measures, intimidation and brutal violence they oversaw the exchange from "mine to ours". When in April 1960 there were only very few private businesses left, the SED appeared satisfied: "Now that all farms have joined the agricultural cooperatives, all the barriers that hindered development in production and raising productivity have been removed."[16] This was the ideological vision, it was part of the "Main Economic Task" and for that reason promised a bright future.

In reality, however, things were once again not following the Marxist-Leninist path. Exactly the opposite of what had been hoped for began to manifest itself. The "Socialist Spring" led to dramatic decreases in production, supply to the whole population noticeably deteriorated and the SED's aggressive claim to power in all aspects of life only served to exasperate the widespread discord between dictatorship and society. The progress seen in the previous years, therefore, was destroyed. Slogans like "Down with Ulbricht" or "Down with the SED"

16 Government statement from 25 April 1960, in: Walter Ulbricht, Die Bauernbefreiung in der Deutschen Demokratischen Republik, Berlin (East) 1962, vol. II, p. 1160.

Flüchtlingszahlen Ost → West
Refugees East → West

Jahr Year	**Flüchtlinge** Refugees	**Übersiedler**[1] Emigrants[1]	**Jahr** Year	**Flüchtlinge** Refugees	**Übersiedler**[1] Emigrants[1]
1949	129.245	–	1978	3.846	8.271
1950	197.788	–	1979	3.512	9.003
1951	165.648	–	1980	3.988	8.775
1952	182.393	–	1981	4.340	11.093
1953	331.390	–	1982	4.095	9.113
1954	184.198	–	1983	3.614	7.729
1955	252.870	–	1984	5.992	34.982
1956	279.189	–	1985	6.160	18.752
1957	261.622	–	1986	6.196	19.982
1958	204.092	–	1987	7.499	11.459
1959	143.917	–	1988	11.893	27.939
1960	199.188	–	bis/till 8.11.1989[2]	241.907	
bis/till 13.8.1961	155.402	–	13.8.61- 8.11.89		
gesamt/total	**2.686.942**		**gesamt/total**	**482.731**	**382.087**
13.8.1961	**Bau der Berliner Mauer** Building of the Berlin Wall		**9.11.89**	**Fall der Berliner Mauer** Fall of the Berlin Wall	
nach/after 13.8.61	51.624	700	nach/after 9.11.89	–	101.947
1962	16.741	4.615	1990	–	395.343
1963	12.967	29.665	1991	–	249.743
1964	11.864	30.012	1992	–	199.170
1965	11.886	17.666	1993	–	172.386
1966	8.456	15.675	1994	–	163.034
1967	6.385	13.188	1995	–	168.336
1968	4.902	11.134	1996	–	166.007
1969	5.273	11.702	1997	–	167.789
1970	5.047	12.472	1998	–	182.478
1971	5.843	11.565	1999	–	195.530
1972	5.537	11.627	2000	–	214.456
1973	6.522	8.667	2001	–	192.002
1974	5.324	7.928	2002	–	176.703
1975	6.011	10.274	2003	–	155.387
1976	5.110	10.058	2004	–	146.352
1977	4.037	8.041	2005	–	137.188
			gesamt nach Mauerfall total after the fall of the Wall		**3.183.851**

^ *It was an expression of the failing politics and remained the central problem for the SED state: the wave of refugees into West Germany.*

were seen increasingly on the sides of buildings in the GDR. The domestic political problems were worsened by the Soviet Union. Khrushchev had caused a clash with the West which climaxed in severe conflict about divided Berlin. Berlin became the focal point of the conflict between the two systems and the "Second Berlin Crisis" became the benchmark of assertiveness for both sides. In 1958, Khrushchev had demanded the withdrawal of all Western troops from the city in order to make it possible to incorporate all of Berlin into the GDR.

When this demand fell on deaf ears, rumours were spreading that "the Russians" might seal off Berlin in order to achieve their goal. In doing so, the last way out of the GDR would have been closed, since the inner German border had already been closed off since 1952. It was only Berlin that remained as a crossover between the two systems due to the allied agreements–and now there was a threat that this may not apply in the future. A real sense of panic set in that this was the last chance to escape–especially in light of the failed SED politics since the fifth Party Conference. There was an explosive increase in the number of people fleeing the GDR. In the summer of 1961, 1,000 people on average were leaving the country every day, on peak days this figure was up to 3,000. The more people who turned their backs on the GDR, the more unstable the GDR became and discussions about the political, economical and social situation became more legitimate. The SED dictatorship was beginning to topple and the party desperately had to react if it wanted to avoid losing power in the near future.

BUILDING OF THE BERLIN WALL

If one was to believe official East German statements, each individual person fleeing the GDR was a class enemy or a traitor, seduced by the materialistic temptations of the decaying capitalist state. These people would not to be missed, said the government. In reality, however, the problem had already been a real threat to existence for quite some time. Those leaving the "Workers' and Peasants' State" were exactly the kind of people the state needed: the well-educated, the young and motivated. In West Germany, by this time, full-time employment was booming and workers were desperately needed. The climate of political unfreedom in the GDR that had intensified to a massive extent since 1956/57 had led to an exodus. In rural areas, entire villages were getting ready to up and leave due to ruthless collectivisation.

Even if it had not been openly acknowledged, the SED leadership had understood for a long time that in order to preserve their dictatorship, the country would have to be completely closed off. While Khrushchev flexed his muscles in a fight with the USA, preparations were being made for what still seemed unlikely: a GDR with closed borders. A high-ranking and secret task force had been in operation since January 1961 and it sought to find a way to end the flow of refugees. Erich Honecker and Erich Mielke were both members. In May, a bewildered Soviet ambassador reported from Berlin to Moscow that the SED was possibly planning to immediately close the sector border to the western side of the city. On the grounds of the allied agreements alone, the East German authorities would not

have been able to do this without permission from the Soviet capital city. This rumour, however, increased pressure on the hegemonic power to make its stance on the question clear. The same was the case for what became probably the most famous scene from the time before the Wall was built. In front of the world's press on 15 June 1961, when Walter Ulbricht pointed out that nobody had any intention of building a wall, decisions had already been made a long time ago. The only thing still missing was permission from the Soviet side.

International developments meant that this permission followed. A summit meeting between Khrushchev and the young American President John F. Kennedy failed at the start of June. Khrushchev once again made demands in regards to Berlin and even threatened war. Kennedy reacted calmly and in the following period made two things clear: if America was infringed upon, then there would be war, which, if necessary would involve the use of nuclear weapons. He also made it clear that there would be no American intervention in affairs to do with the Soviet Occupation Zone. In regards to West Berlin, he announced his "Three Essentials": the presence of Western troops in Berlin, free access to the city and the guarantee that the people would survive. As long as these were adhered to, there would be no American intervention.

^ *Press conference, 15 June 1961. Walter Ulbricht unwittingly says "Nobody has the intention of building a wall."*

The last barrier had now fallen. Building a wall would not violate any of Kennedy's essentials. The Soviets could assume with all probability that there would be no military confrontation if they were to go ahead and build a wall.

Since the SED leadership had been communicating to Moscow for the past year that the GDR would not exist much longer if it were not sealed off from West Berlin, Khrushchev complied. The decisive words were spoken during a conversation on 3 August 1961. Ulbricht noted: "Flight from GDR great. Administrative actions: close border."[17] Reasons for constructing the Wall were given immediately: the Cold War, class enemies and the defence of the GDR against foreign enemies. On 3 August, however, the truth was revealed: the reason for closing the border was the stream of refugees leaving the country—and that was a result of the SED's catastrophic politics. In 16 years, the illegitimate rulers, despite their actions, had failed to find a majority, and now the people had to be walled in to ensure the dictatorship's future. Honecker was responsible for implementing everything and, in the next few days, he would live up to his role as Ulbricht's crown prince and command himself to higher things.

17 Matthias Uhl/Armin Wagner (Ed.), Ulbricht, Chruschtschow und die Mauer. Eine Dokumentation, Munich 2003, p. 93.

^ *While Khrushchev (left) and Kennedy (right) are still negotiating, Ulbricht is making preparations to block off West Berlin.*

After the landmark decision had been made, everything went very fast. The preparations paid off. In the following days, almost all leading committees from party and state came together, and it was as though they were approving the next steps of action which had long since been decided on. However, almost nobody recognised, or wanted to recognise, exactly what was going on. There was obscure talk of "decided measures" and "necessary provisions", nobody mentioned the building of a wall.

And then it happened. During the night of 12 to 13 August 1961, members of the People's Police, border police, Combat Group of the Working Class and troops from the National People's Army moved in along the 160 kilometre long external border to West Berlin. The Red Army remained in the background, as had been agreed. Blocking off West Berlin began: road links were blocked, local public transport was capped, ditches were dug and barbed wire was erected. The majority of Berliners were sleeping in their beds while world history was taking place on their streets.

Indeed, there had been discussions at the time about the possibility of cordoning off certain areas, but nobody could

^ *Putting up the border exactly where the first part of the Wall would later fall. Uniformed services erect provisional barricades on Bornholmer Straße.*

have imagined that it would be possible to divide a dynamic, vibrant metropolis steeped in history like Berlin.

However, it turned out that this was within the realms of possibility. West Berlin was now an island in the middle of the GDR.

There was, however, an element of uncertainty and the SED paid attention to it immediately. It was fairly certain that the Americans would not intervene, but how would the people react? As would later emerge, they reacted with incomprehen-

^ *There is still no wall to be seen, but connections between East and West are cut throughout the city.*

sion and few public protests–but above all, with bewilderment. Those who still wanted to and still could took the last opportunity to flee the "Workers' and Peasants' State". On the 13 August alone, there were more than 100 escapes over the border. Two days later, it was twice as many. 19 year old police officer Conrad Schumann became the symbol of the acts of desperation. On 15 August, wearing his uniform and with his weapon in his hand, he leapt over the barbed wire on Bernauer Straße towards West Berlin.

Those in power considered sealing off West Berlin as a quick, effective and satisfactory success. The ongoing refugees, however, jeopardised everything: cordoning off the West only made sense if it was done outright. That meant being prepared to use any means necessary. It is profoundly inhumane, but was logical in terms of power: those who wanted the Wall would have to allow shots to be fired. To that effect, on 22 August an act was passed by the SED Politburo. There had already been refugees who had lost their lives while trying to escape, but the first deadly shots were fired as early as 24 August. They were not to be the final shots. The martial construction would ultimately claim at least 184 lives.

The people's belief that these measures would not be long-term, the rapid extension of the border fortifications, the killing of refugees and the general repression throughout the GDR only led to inconsequential protests against these feared

^ *The most famous escapee: Conrad Schumann jumps over the barbed wire. He feared SED revenge for the rest of his life.*

B.Z.
Extrablatt
Seit heute früh:
BLOCKADE
über Ost-Berlin
verhängt!
Panzer an allen Grenzen
Stacheldraht um Sowjetsektor
Verbot für alle Grenzgänger
Interzonenverkehr normal

radical actions. They came to nothing. On 13 August, the SED had brought its power to a new level. The question was what it would do with it.

^ *The unimaginable has happened. Nobody knows it at this time, but it will last 28 years. Berlin is divided.*

ACHT
Sie verl
WEST

^ *"Attention! You are now leaving West Berlin."*

^ *Armed officers look towards the West. They can see the growing protests around the Brandenburg Gate.*

^ *The Combat Groups stand at the front. All the other units are in the background, but nevertheless present.*

^ *The dividing line is quickly expanded. Direct contact over the border is still possible, but this changes quickly.*

S
U

^ *The dividing line is quickly expanded. Direct contact over the border is still possible, but this changes quickly.*

S
U

^ *Between meetings and divisions, waiting and escaping—personal and world history was being made.*

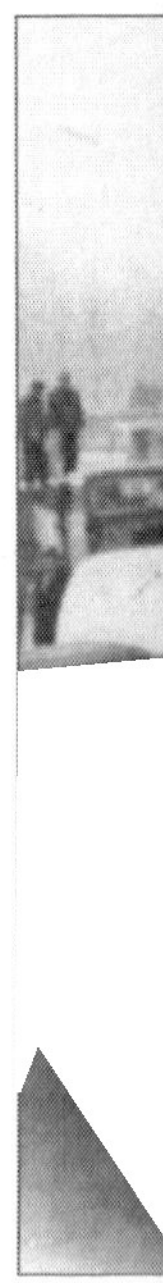

^ *It quickly became clear to see that the SED leaders were serious. The deadly border was continually expanded until 1989.*

^ *Three months later. The aerial photos from November 1961 show how deep the divide in Berlin had already become.*

3 MAY 1971
FROM ULBRICHT TO HONECKER

ARRANGEMENTS BEHIND THE WALL

The harsh period of repression that followed after the Wall was built continued well into 1962. On the one hand, the SED leaders considered it necessary to overcome any resistance to the path already taken, and on the other hand, to continue to change the general framework to suit their own aims.

There was no people's uprising after 13 August, but that did not mean that all was calm behind the Wall. In many parts of the country, leaflets began to spread which criticised the martial construction. People made their negative feelings towards the establishing system known. Scenes of rebellion against collectivisation continued to play out in small villages. Above average numbers of soldiers were deserting from the army. Strike threats were on the increase. Despite those who had been shot, the amount of escape attempts did not go down. SED representatives also claimed time and time again to be discovering the worst imaginable thing possible for guardians of communist morals: "political-ideological diversion". This vague term encompassed all political views that differed from theirs and, in their opinion, these views could always be traced back to negative influences from the West and were considered to be the nucleus of the opposition. Therefore, it was concluded, such views had to be suppressed. Erich Mielke, head of East Germany's Ministry for State Security, made it unequivocally clear how these people were to be dealt with, "Those who turn up with enemy solutions are to be arrested. Enemies are to be dealt with harshly and in these times, even more so".[18]

18 Staff meeting protocol on 11 August 1961, in: BStU, ZAIG, no. 4.900, Bl. 3.

This was not without consequence: the number of arrests exploded again. The Stasi had arrested 280 people in July 1961, by August it was already 1,093 and a further 970 in September. Prisons in the GDR were filling up. The number of inmates in the second half of the year rose from 25,000 to approximately 40,000. Now, since the border had been closed for good and the people had been denied the last route out, it appeared that the time had come to reprimand all those who did not avow themselves completely to socialism and the SED dictatorship. A rule of force prevailed in many regions of the country. Officials beat up young people, they threatened respectable members of the public, carried out random arrests, confiscated valuable consumer goods and abused their positions in order to settle personal accounts. On some occasions, superior members of the party felt compelled to intervene and put a stop to the rampant lawlessness.

The extent to which the state and the party felt compelled to adhere to their own laws in the months after the Wall was built became brutally clear on 3 October 1961. There were countless tragedies on that day along the inner German border between Kreis Grevesmühlen near the coast of the Baltic Sea to Vogtland (an area which reaches across Bavaria, Saxony and Thuringia). The trigger for the events was the planned "Aktion Festigung" (Action Consolidation). It had been ordered by the

^ *Everything seems normal. While a wave of arrests makes its way across the country, propaganda offered well-known slogans.*

central body and planned with military precision. It served to bring life in the closed off areas of the country into line with SED expectations, more so than it had previously been and also to prevent the escape of its own people more effectively. In order to achieve this, a strip of land, five kilometre wide, was cleared along the inner-German border. Whoever was deemed to be politically unreliable, or even those who were considered merely suspicious, suffered the same fate on 3 October 1961: these residents were informed that they were to change their residence for their own safety and for the safety of the border. However, in most cases, lorries, guarded by armed men, pulled up 30 minutes later to clear the houses. There was only one option for those concerned: to comply unconditionally with these measures and accept their new assigned homes, or to protest, and in most cases, lose both their property and their freedom. Suddenly, more than 3,000 people, among them 1,000 children, had to leave their homes unprepared and without an alternative; there was no possibility to object and it was no longer possible to escape to the West. The operation killed two birds with one stone. The border region was now secure and a violent and clear message had been sent to citizens of the GDR: on 13 August 1961, any sense of reservation had disappeared and the SED would stoop to any level in order to cement its power.

There were, of course, also people who saw a chance in these new circumstances. Among them were those who had linked their careers, their status and their future with the party. At long last, they argued, a clear system prevailed and the SED's objectives could be implemented without interruption. However, one did not have to necessarily be communist to come to such conclusions. Even those who considered themselves primarily apolitical, as well as those who got by and even those who achieved modest prosperity, they all frequently tended to at least silently accept the building of the Wall. For them, the Wall was symbolic of hopes for a rosy future. All too often, they closed their eyes to the barbaric aspects of the rigorous state division. Furthermore, the anti-fascist myth surrounding the GDR's foundation continued to be effective. It was no coincidence that the regime glorified the Wall as an "Anti-Fascist Protection Rampart". This interpretation offered something positive to all those who considered the GDR to be the better half of Germany; measures to break away from the National Socialist past were supposedly only taken in the GDR. Fundamentally, the relentless propaganda had the desired effect and kept the reality of the situation hidden from a relevant proportion of the population.

All in all, there was a wide mix of opinions behind the Wall, from active resistance to declarations of approval and everything in between. At the same time, at least for fellow citizens close to the system, they would have shared Christa Wolf's view. Wolf retrospectively wrote:

> "In Halle, I felt a sense of relief in the workshop when the borders were closed. Before this, one had to fear that the workshop was going to be stripped of its engineers and skilled workers. It was said among management that now there was no intervention from the outside, people would talk more openly and honestly with each other. People would once again be able to be openly critical. "[19]

Despite the repressive measures in place, there were still some signs of hope that it would once again be possible after the building of the Wall for people to express and voice their opinions, and hence, pave the way for a greater level of tolerance. It was of great symbolic significance that by November 1961, the person who had cast an oppressive shadow over the country had since disappeared from public space: Stalin. The Soviet dictator had been dead for over ten years and critical assessments about him had even been made in his own country. It was only in the GDR that his cult of personality had survived unscathed. In order to put an end to this, monuments were silently torn down, streets named after him were given new names, and Stalinstadt was suddenly called Eisenhüttenstadt. These measures could be regarded as an awakening during a time of enlightenment.

It is also indicative that the SED leadership began to make apologetic concessions to its people, introduce further means

19 Christa Wolf, Ein Tag im Jahr 1960–2000, Munich 2003, p. 46.

of identification and wake hope for the future. While young men were still hit hard by the introduction of conscription—a step which had been unthinkable before the building of the Wall—the party was giving more importance to the role of women than had ever been seen before. Equal rights for women was effectively made a state objective. In reality, however, this was never implemented. On a cultural level, things appeared to be thawing again in 1962. At the end of the year, for example, the still young Wolf Biermann, who had emigrated from West to East-Germany, was allowed to officially recite his critical poetry at the Berlin Academy of Arts. By this time, almost 16,000 prisoners had been freed since June. There was a breeze of liberality in the air and it was to grow even stronger.

ECONOMIC REFORM EFFORTS

From 1962/63, SED reforms were most noticeable in the economy. New ground was broken and the population felt this on a large scale. At no other time in the GDR were there greater efforts made towards economical reform. The resulting changes were a fundamental feature of the sixties.

Those in power had been trying hard to introduce an all encompassing controlled economy since the end of the Second World War. In doing so, according to the ideological fundamental conviction, the uncertainties of the marketplace would be neutralised, supply and demand would be matched and the material needs of the people would largely be met. In reality, however, things looked very different. Nationalising the industrial sector put a stop to its sustainable development and collectivisation of the agricultural sector led to dramatic drops in yield. The GDR was lagging far behind in terms of the economical competition with West Germany. The same could be said for the overall standard of living. It seemed that even the SED's leaders were beginning to see that things could not continue as they were. Behind the Wall, the SED set about finding innovative solutions to the problems that had been building up. The fact that these problems, as well as the dynamics that were setting in, had actually been caused by the inadequacies in their own politics, in particular as a result of the economic crisis in 1960/61, was hard for some of the leaders to see. This fact was completely covered up by the continuing propaganda. There was a wide-spread mood of change in the air and 1962 was a year which was shaped among other things by extensive and

relative open discussions about how the GDR's economy was to move forward. Firstly, the SED leaders took the opinions of qualified professionals into consideration. Equipped with the instincts of a radical power politician, Ulbricht now took to leading the debate. In January 1963, the official go-ahead for the upcoming changes was then given, as is so often the case in the history of the GDR, at an SED party conference. It passed legislation on the "New Economic System" (NÖS), the aim of which was to create a more modern, more dynamic and, thereby, more efficient economy. The GDR's economy should finally reach a level at which it was able to compete internationally and win itself a solid place on the global market. The crucial medium needed to achieve this: further implementation of half-market economy elements. Companies were to be given more control from then on in order to better determine their own profit, which would create material incentives for workers and increase productivity. Many things now seemed possible and the economy in the "Workers' and Peasants' State" was a sort of laboratory in which its superiority over capitalism should be proved. Every single citizen of the GDR, according to the promise, was to benefit. And, indeed, the change did bring about positive effects very quickly: in 1964 production had already noticeably increased and so had wages.

^ *May 1963. The division of Berlin becomes part of everyday life. Life in the GDR goes on. This will only continue for a limited period.*

However, the euphoria was short-lived. The reason for this was that the reform was ultimately geared towards a *non-economical* aim: safeguarding the SED dictatorship. Politics once again was above the economy and the boundaries for change were very limited right from the start. Companies were indeed told they had personal responsibility, but this was quickly suppressed as it posed a threat to the existing system. Elements of market economy should be introduced, but at the same time, the market economy continued to be stigmatised as an essential feature of capitalism, which was allegedly dying. It is true that the SED leaders had consulted experts during the preparation and implementation of the reform, but their responsibility ended as soon as they had given their opinions. In short, the reforms were inconsequential, subject to the priority of politics, and were only accepted by those in power as long as their positions were not subsequently threatened. Failure of the reforms was, therefore, inevitable.

Erich Apelt, a high-ranking economics SED official and head of the National Planning Committee (SPK), became a tragic symbol of this failure. He had made major contributions to the developments which had been unthinkable until this point and had already come under fire in 1965 when it became clear that the reforms were not going to fulfil their expectations in light of the aforementioned inadequacies. This brought orthodox communist hardliners on to the scene, among them Erich Honecker, who warned of consequences beyond control if an overly liberal economic policy was introduced. They were still unable to assert power, but there was a divide growing between Honecker and his political mentor, Ulbricht. The reforms gradually came into disrepute and it was for this reason, among others, that Apelt took his own life in December 1965.

The general willingness of the SED to tolerate a climate of social change towards openness grew weaker from the mid-1960s. That was also refelcted in the economy. The "New Economic System" was gradually withdrawn and rigid central control took over once more. With the help of the NÖS, it had been possible to improve the standard of living for the entire population, but this method proved to be an increasing strain on the country's very foundations. By the end of the decade, there were more and more signs that pointed towards a loom-

ing crisis which then happened in 1969/70. Cooperation between companies was no longer working, due simply to the lack of materials and replacement equipment. This breakdown in production led to drastic results for the people: "Above all there were not enough warm undergarments, warm clothes for children, or warm sports clothes. There were not enough winter shoes, batteries, furniture, household goods, toothbrushes or spark plugs."[20] After a quarter of a century under SED rule and seven years of economic reforms, there were still shortages of the most basic things. That was the end of the reforms, it strengthened the position for the conservatives in the SED and would quickly prove to be an important factor in the end of Ulbricht's era.

20 André Steiner, Von Plan zu Plan. Eine Wirtschaftsgeschichte der DDR, Berlin 2007, p. 182.

^ *March 1964. Walter Ulbricht visits the Leipzig Trade Fair. On the left, Erich Apel, the tragic figure of the GDR's economic history.*

ONE STEP FORWARD, TWO STEPS BACK

For the GDR, the 1960s were a decade in which a great deal seemed possible in many other areas also outside of the economy, and welcome reform was in the air. Rarely had the all-powerful SED signalled so much readiness to modify its own politics. This was a seemingly open-ended situation (in a country where nothing was left open-ended). If nothing else, this led to citizens being able to identify with the efforts for reform, and artists and intellectuals very much led the way. This did not, however, mean that they agreed with the all-powerful party, nor did they agree with the dictatorship the party had created. A prevailing mood of optimism about the future of the GDR was, however, beginning to spread. Even today, many contemporary witnesses are transfigured when they look back at this time–their conclusions about this period are therefore nostalgic and false. What was valid for the economy, was valid for everything. The SED did accept change, but only if it remained in boundaries which the SED defined. Self-fulfilment, freedom of speech and democracy were not part of the plan. It would become apparent very quickly that tolerance had by no means found a place in the self-proclaimed "Workers' and Peasants' State".

And yet it had seemed as though this would be the case at the start of the decade, after the repression had died down immediately after the construction of the Wall. Although it would later be proved to be nothing more than a pretence, the party approached its people again and tried once more to win them

over. And what could be more important than securing the approval of the young? Their particular significance for the future of the GDR was emphasised relentlessly. The SED canvassed for the young more than ever before. What had previously been unimaginable was now becoming reality; the quest to win support reached its climax in September 1963 with an official announcement that seemed to determine future youth policies in the GDR. Using the motto "Give youth trust and responsibility", the aim was to abolish aggressive heteronomy. Suddenly there was talk of "thinking and acting for yourself", of an end of "lack of understanding and patronising", even of "(more) equal rights". This was new, this was exciting and at the same time it was ambiguous. Exactly where all this supposed freedom should lead to had been clearly defined:

> "From you, the boys and girls in the German Democratic Republic, a lot is required: based on more than one hundred years of the German workers movement tradition (...) you will help to establish the German future in

^ *German National Youth Conference in Berlin, May 1964. There are cheers for party and state leaders on the VIP stand.*

> the GDR. It has now become clear to every independent thinking young person that the future of Germany lies only in a socialist order."[21]

In the midst of an atmosphere of change in the early 1960s, the true meaning and implications of this were overlooked: anyone who did not declare themselves to socialism unconditionally—and therefore to the SED—was automatically considered retrogressive and would have to reckon with harsh consequences. Just a few years later, the concrete consequences of this would become apparent.

The extent to which those in power really understood the facts of life became clear in one other area: culture. At the end of the 1950s, before the Wall was built, there had been an unlikely development in the GDR: workers, artists and writers had approached each other, mingled with each other and looked to understand each other's roles. This was again a politically staged and naïve attempt by the SED leaders to create a culture of socialism which would be superior to any civil attempts. Its motto was "Greif zur Feder, Kumpel!" (Grab your pen, miner!). In some cases, it fell on sympathetic ears, but its results were far from impressive. Nevertheless, a lot was possible in the cultural sector during this relatively liberal period.

Mildly critical novels like Erwin Strittmatter's "Ole Bienkopp" were published, films including "Spur der Steine" (Trace

21 Neues Deutschland, 21 September 1963, pages 1-3, here p. 2.

^ *A socialist cultural staging. A writer's conference at Elektrochemischen Kombinat Bitterfeld (a chemical industry complex in Bitterfeld, East Germany) on 24 April 1959.*

of Stones), which gave a more realistic depiction of daily life than had previously been seen, were filmed, and beat music, which had once been frowned upon, enjoyed growing popularity which was no longer condemned.

However, at the sixth party conference in January 1963, the mild disapproval towards this liberality was already becoming more intense and continued to grow in the period that followed. Against the backdrop of the "New Economic System", intra-party tensions about the extent to which such developments should be tolerated were eased. With considerable support from Honecker, critics increasingly prevailed. Openness towards culture was officially over once and for all in December 1965. At an SED party leader conference, with the infamous "11th Plenum", the wind changed direction. Honecker emphasised that the GDR was a "clean" state in which there was no place for decadent trends, especially not if they were from the West. Scores of writers were reprimanded as a result, their books banned and films prohibited. Brigitte Reimann, an up-and-coming young writer at the time, recorded in her diary: "Honecker's speech from the 11th Plenum was printed today. The cat is out of the bag: writers are to blame for the moral brutalisation of the young." That was the end of steps towards liberal culture and youth politics. Reimann: "It makes me wanna puke".[22]

The fact that the orthodox SED powers were able to prevail was down to two things. Since the People's Uprising in 1953, the overwhelming majority of party officials feared nothing more than the uncontrollable consequences of a tolerant

22 Brigitte Reimann, Alles schmeckt nach Abschied. Tagebücher 1964-1970, Berlin 1998, p. 170.

^ *Momentous as ever. The sixth SED Party Conference gives clear signals that the open-minded approach towards culture would soon be over.*

attitude towards exercising power. It had also been proved in Hungary in 1956 what this could lead to. Therefore, caution was required. Furthermore, the wind had also changed in Moscow: Khrushchev had fallen from power in 1964 and all important party and state officials had been relieved of there positions. Leonid Brezhnev became his successor, a communist hardliner. He made it unmistakeably clear that any kind of attempt at reform that did not completely comply with Marxist-Leninist ideals would not be tolerated. Honecker and his followers could be sure of his support and ultimately won the showdown with Ulbricht. The dynamics of the previous years slowed down drastically and eventually culminated in Honecker's strictly regimented era.

Besides, even the tolerance in the superficially liberal years was constricted by the aforementioned tight limits. While the SED projected an image of a modern party, behind the scenes, it carried on working on consolidating power in an almost Stalin-like fashion. Indeed, the period of open and brutal combat against both real and alleged enemies had come to an end, but in return hidden repression was on the increase. For this reason, the Stasi–who referred to itself as the party's "sword and shield" and whose power was exerted with all imaginable means–experienced dramatic growth. The number of staff almost doubled from around 23,000 in 1960 to over 43,000 in 1970. Likewise, the existing structure behind it was extended, differentiated and fitted to its respective circumstances. Similar actions were taken in other security bodies: from the vigorous and impelled expansion of the National People's Army (NVA), to the installation of a comprehensive net of community police, right through to a general militarisation of society. The Combat Group of the Working Class kept workers ready for defence, the Sport and Technology Association (GST) concentrated on the young, and even women could now be seen in military propaganda. And, during the 1960s, whenever it was deemed necessary, those in

power did not shy from securing their totalitarian regime by using all means necessary and at times resorted to most inhumane methods. In August 1962, Peter Fechter was shot on the East German border at the Berlin Wall. As he lay, bleeding to death, assistance that could have been given was not rendered. In the mid-1960s, the number of critics being banned from their professions or from public appearances was on the rise. This was even the case for those who did not challenge socialism, including singer-songwriter, Wolf Biermann, and philosopher, Robert Havemann. In GDR villages, landowners were forced to join larger agricultural cooperatives–and also to pay for doing so. The new penal code from 1967 did signal a certain amount of progression, but at the same time defined the duty of law to be the "protection of the socialist state and social order". Political criminal offences, therefore, continued to apply and could be avenged with tough sentences extending right through to the death penalty.

In many regards, the year 1968 proved to be a radical year. The GDR received a new constitution for the first time since its foundation in October 1949. It cemented the existing prevalent situation and, at the same time, revealed how far fact and fiction had already grown apart. Even the first article addressed the SED's unshakable leadership role and socialism as the state's highest priorities. At the same time, and strikingly contradictory, there was talk of freedom of conscience, freedom of

^ *Pictures that went around the world. Peter Fechter bleeds to death on the death strip. A memorial stands here today.*

faith, freedom of press and opinion. Article 54 spoke of "free, public and confidential votes", which had last existed to a certain extent in 1946. Since then, using a voting booth had been frowned upon and everyone knew that doing so could result in negative consequences for one's career, family and existence. But, for the "development of the socialist collective human community", as was referred to in article 18, this was irrelevant. GDR citizens had to show insight into supposedly objective requirements which defined the party. Those who did not, had to reckon with the consequences–what was printed in the constitution was of little help in such a case. It created a make-

believe world, daily life had been very different for a long time.

Just how far apart fact and fiction now were would be highlighted as the year went on. Neighbouring Czechoslovakia had also resorted to reform efforts as it also suffered from a list of problems. Unlike the GDR, the reforms here were not broken one by one, but went on to gain more and more strength until they culminated in an attempt to give socialism a "human face". Socialism and democracy should be in harmony with each other–that was like squaring the circle. GDR citizens closely followed the developments during the "Prague Spring" (as it has gone down in history) as they hoped that democracy would also be possible in their country. Any such hope was brutally dashed on 20 August 1968. In the early evening, a Soviet-led military operation by various Eastern block armies invaded. During the night, the troops occupied Czechoslovakia and the movement for reform was bloodily quelled. Once more, the fear of consequences beyond control had been the cause for the eruption. The GDR was denied permission to join in on the aggression, even though both Ulbricht and Honecker made every effort to do so: the notion of German tanks rolling through Prague again was too alarming even for Leonid Brezhnev.

The message behind the events in the Czech capital was unmistakeable, it was also devastating. The reformers there had been communists and had merely tried to brighten up the dreariness of socialism, not to abolish it. However, even that was too much and was beyond the parameters of what was deemed to be acceptable by Moscow. The inevitable consequence of this was the disappearance of a "human face" in the

GDR. Reform and socialism, democracy and socialism, these two things—as the events in Prague had shown all too clearly—did not go together. Despite the material improvement of everyday life, life was dull and, given the current circumstances, the future offered little reason for hope. This resulted in a widespread apathy which grew over the GDR and its people like a layer of mildew. However, this apathy was to be disturbed once more—by the most unlikely of candidates.

^ *Prague, 21 August 1968. Soviet tanks move into the city and crush the reform efforts bloodily.*

WALTER ULBRICHT'S REMOVAL

Where does this kind of thing happen? Politicians in the West step down or sit on the sidelines after losing an election. Politicians in the East fall or die," an excerpt from the West German political supplement in early May 1971. "For the people of both German states, Walter Ulbricht was for almost twenty years (...) the most underestimated, most hated man, a caricature and creature with ludicrous features." The Author went on to say that, in his opinion, a lot had changed in regard to this in the last few years, and that Ulbricht had gained everyone's "respect"[23]. This assessment may well have been shared by only a minority of GDR citizens, but it did not matter anymore: Ulbricht's time was over.

When the SED's Central Committee met in East Berlin on 3 May 1971, there was no public indication that fundamental changes were ahead. Hardly anyone was capable of thinking that the party would do anything groundbreaking at this point in time. The end of the last decade had been too sobering. Thousands had shown their rejection of the current climate by finding a way to the West despite the closed borders. Ulbricht had defined the political events of the day since the end of the Second World War, firstly only in the background and then as the most influential statesman. Neither the Western press, nor the East German people thought this would change in the near future but they were to be proved wrong. A few days before it was officially made public, an announcement was

23 DER SPIEGEL Nr. 20/1971, 10 May 1971, p. 34.

made to those in the SED's innermost circle of power and the Politburo that Ulbricht had to give up his leadership position. This was a tricky situation since there were no rules in the communist movement in relation to such a move. So, the successor had instigated a palace revolution. Ultimately, there was one reason behind its success: it had been given the go-ahead by Moscow. By then, Ulbricht's politics were under increasing scrutiny and his ways were considered to be unpredictable. The failed attempts at reform in the 1960s, the failed attempt to overtake the West German economy, single-handed efforts towards the East German-West German relations and a certain stubbornness–even towards his Soviet comrade–meant that Brezhnev was prepared to take a radical step. Ulbricht's crown prince had already been urging the removal of his political mentor for months and it was now time: the man who had spent more than a quarter of a century in control of the self-proclaimed "Workers' and Peasants' State" resigned without so much as a whimper. Furthermore, he had to officially request to be relieved of his duties as First Secretary of the Central Committee "on grounds of age". He also had to put the name of his scheming successor forward: Erich Honecker. Formally, as Chairman of the State Council for East Germany, he did remain head of state but, in reality, all power had been stripped from him. He ceased to make public appearances,

^ *Moscow's new leader, Leonid Brezhnev, visits the GDR in April 1967. The bond with Ulbricht does not last long.*

he was not mentioned in the media and, until his death on 1 August 1973, he lived a secluded and withdrawn lifestyle. He was even forgotten quickly by his own party–this was encouraged by his successor.

With Honecker's enthronement (Honecker already being 58 at this point), it was apparent that changes were to take place. The new strongman shared many of the same experiences with the former: he came from a modest background, had been affiliated with the Communist movement from an early age, had lived through Nazi barbarity and had been behind the change in course since 1945. He was a man of the political machine, a full-time official with a stellar party career. He was chairman of the Free German Youth (FDJ) when the GDR was formed, had supported Ulbricht after the People's Uprising and subsequently rose into the highest party positions during the 1950s. His baptism of fire had been the building of the Wall: as the secretary of the Central Committee, he had been in charge of organisations. The SED (and Moscow) thought that he had carried out this duty with great success and, as a result, he commended himself to the highest office. On the other side of the SED, Honecker was appreciated to a lesser extent–he was mostly considered a faint bureaucrat with limited possibilities. Nevertheless, when he saw his chance coming at the end of the 1960s, he made every effort to overthrow Ulbricht. He had

^ *A bureaucrat working inconspicuously but with great determination on his career: Erich Honecker. Here in 1951 as leader of the Free German Youth (FDJ).*

learned this from his predecessor, who also never hesitated to get rid of political competition. On 3 May 1971, Honecker climbed to the top of the power pyramid. The only question was what would happen next.

^ *Deprived of power. Ulbricht is discharged in June 1971. Outwardly, however, he must appear content, like here while greeting communists from Prague.*

144

^ *On target. Honecker is officially inaugurated in June 1971 at the eighth party congress. He rules over the GDR until 1989.*

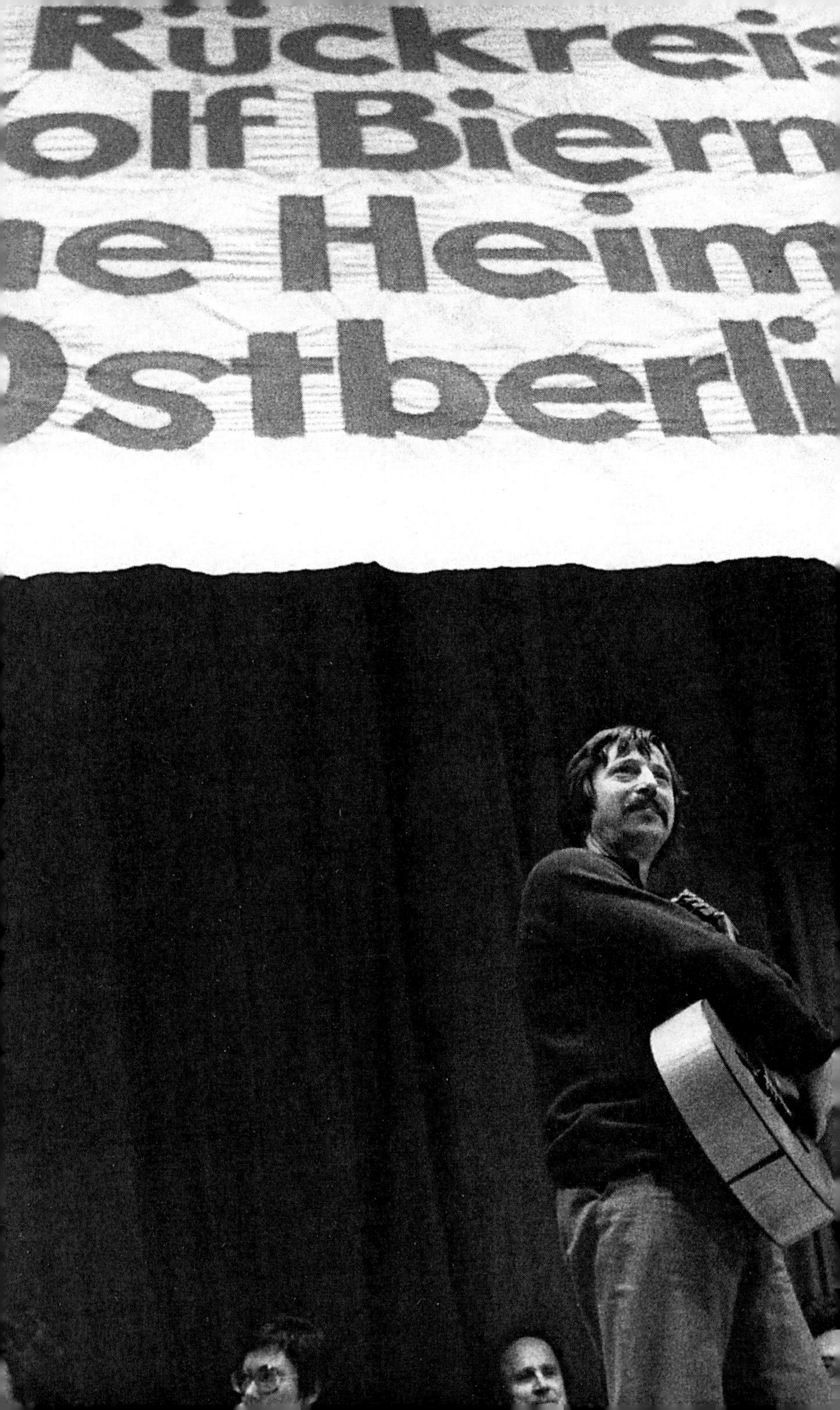
Rückreis
olf Bierm
ie Heim
Ostberli

16 NOVEMBER 1976

BIERMANN AND THE CONSEQUENCES

A NEW "MAIN TASK"

Once again, it was during a party conference (the eighth) that the path for the next series of events was paved. There was great uncertainty within the party. What consequences would the surprising change of power have and in which direction would things go now? Honecker was not stuck for an answer to these questions for long. Already in June 1971, only a few weeks after the palace revolution which he had initiated, he appeared in the East Berlin Werner-Seelenbinder-Halle, stood at the lectern and announced his visions for the future.

What he had to say made people sit up and listen. After a decade which aimed to modernise and grow the industrial sector, it was now time to return to the needs of the people: the "material and cultural enhancement in the people's living standards" was declared as the new "main task"[24] for all politics.

That was a fundamental break from the Ulbricht years and a radical change for the SED's (economic) policy. If until now the supreme aim had been to achieve an internationally competitive economy in order to take the second step towards improving the standard of living in the GDR, the opposite approach was now being put in place. First of all, the citizen's material situation had to be noticeably improved. This, according to the conviction, would awaken their enthusiasm for socialism like never before and would lead to higher productivity in all other areas of life. Loyalty was to generate stability. In

24 VIII. SED Party Conference negotiations protocol, vol. 1, Berlin (East) 1971, p. 61.

other words: money had to be spent first, this would lead to more commitment, which would in turn lead to high takings. What the new strongman failed to mention: the desired positive effects could only be achieved if both points were met to the fullest extent. If this was not the case, due to its increased expenditure on consumption and social political measures, the GDR would inevitably fall deeper and deeper into debt.

Honecker's new definition of the "main task" went down in history as the "unity of economic and social policy" (Einheit von Wirtschafts- und Sozialpolitik) and quickly delivered, on the whole, initially pleasing results. Never before had there been a time in the history of the GDR in which living conditions improved so widespread and so quickly. Until the

^ *Recovery. Implosion-resistant cathode-ray tubes (used in televisions) are presented in Leipzig. Relaxation is the order of the day at Müggelsee, a lake in Berlin.*

middle of the 1970s, wages and pensions were repeatedly raised, and low-earners especially profited from this. The average income was also raised: from 755 East German Marks in 1970, to 850 Marks four years later. Holiday entitlement was raised as weekly working hours were decreased. Young families were now able to take advantage of interest-free loans and the amount of paid maternity leave following the birth of a child was extended. Full-time employment ruled in the "Workers' and Peasants' State" and the prices for staple foods remained stable, despite increasing prices on the global market.

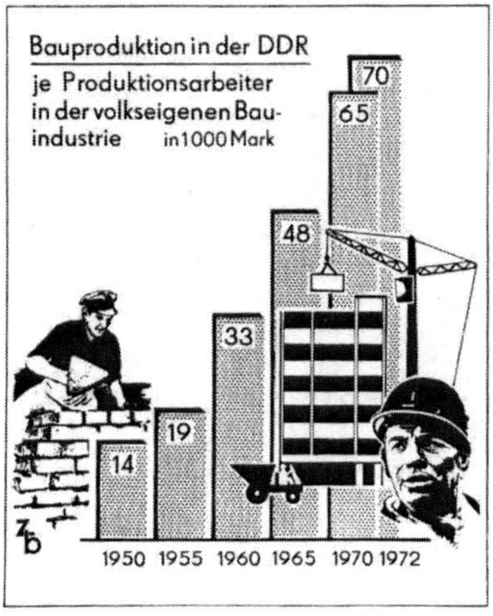

At the heart of the "unity of economic and social policy" was a residential building programme. It was clear that there were still huge problems in terms of housing and this "social question" would have to be dealt with by 1990. By 1975, plans to build 500,000 homes were made, the number would

^ *There is a boom in construction. Both residential and prestigious buildings are constructed, like here on Alexanderplatz, Berlin.*

eventually amount to almost three million. Indeed, construction was undertaken at a brisk rate. The strategic focus, on the other hand, was soon recognisable: in industrial construction it was necessary to build as many buildings as possible, as quickly as possible and as inexpensively as possible. In both small communities and on the outskirts of larger cities, new constructions were springing out of the ground: the "Platte" (prefabricated building made from concrete slabs) quickly be-

^ *Entire city districts and functional buildings seem to grow out of the ground, like Marzahn in Berlin, and the city's sport and recreation centre.*

came synonymous with construction sites. The inner-cities and village centres, on the other hand, were more run-down than before. On the whole, however, the progress achieved between 1972 and 1975 was considerable. Shops were filled with items

^ *Zest for life spreads across the nation, from the beaches at the Baltic Sea to the amusement park at Plänterwald.*

which had previously not been available, people's savings grew disproportionately and there was a rapid rise in the amount of made-to-last goods being purchased. According to official records, 15 percent of households owned a car in 1970, and this figure doubled by 1976. In the same period, the percentage of households that owned a fridge leapt from 65 percent to 89 percent, and those that owned washing machines rose from 58 percent to 83 percent. Similar developments in terms of per capita consumption were also recorded. There was no doubt about it, the GDR was moving upwards, everyday life was becoming easier and the future seemed worth striving for.

The fact that hardship was impending, despite all of these positive indicators, became apparent in the mid-1970s. Productivity and the volume of production had grown in both industry and agriculture, even the economic lag behind West Germany seemed to be getting smaller. Such growth, however, was not enough to offset ever increasing costs; loans from Western states had to close the growing hole. The SED continually gave its people new socio-political acquisitions, it did it on a big scale—however, it certainly could not afford to. Serious consequences soon became apparent. These consequences turned out to be even more severe when the new SED leaders decided to get rid of what remained of the private sector in 1971/72. At this time, more than 10 percent of the GDR's gross

^ *Self-service department stores were built everywhere. They also profited long-term from the increasing range of goods.*

output was generated by private businesses which were not, or only in part, nationalised. They were mostly smaller businesses which were often highly specialised and produced rare consumer goods. They were economically successful and staff earned substantially more than in the publicly owned sector. These companies, however, had one major defect: they were simply not envisaged in Marxist-Leninist ideology. They had been tolerated until now, since they had an important role to play in supplying the nation. But Honecker decided—also in order to differentiate himself from his predecessor—that their time had come to an end. Almost 11,000 companies, varying in type, were subsequently expropriated, bought up and nationalised; at best, the owners received a very small amount of financial compensation. As had already been seen, ideological motives tipped the scales. His moves had nothing to do with economic rationality, but matched the reality of those in power. This, once more, was the deciding factor.

^ *The Berlin TV Tower has been symbolic of GDR accomplishment since 1969. It is still a popular attraction today.*

BETWEEN CONFIDENCE AND RESIGNATION

Anyone who wishes to understand the GDR's dramatic downfall at the end of the 1980s not only has to take its founding mistakes into consideration, but also the growing (and ultimately bitterly dashed) hope of Honecker's era. It was not just the general living standards that improved dramatically; it finally looked like the "Workers' and Peasants' State" was moving up. As regards to foreign policy, there was a string of successes: the GDR joined UNESCO in 1972. In May 1973, the GDR became a member of the World Health Organisation (WHO) and in September of the same year–at the same time as West Germany–also a full member of the United Nations (UN). Those in power had fought long and hard for international recognition, and that had now been achieved.

However, developments were not only global: bilateral agreements were abundant. At the start of 1973, 13 (predominantly Western) states established diplomatic relationships with the GDR, among them Italy, Spain and the Netherlands. Shortly after, Britain and France followed. The USA then followed in September 1974. The GDR, precariously founded and never democratically legitimate, was on the way to becoming an important partner in the global community. The GDR never missed an opportunity to celebrate this. In doing so, it aimed to establish loyalty from its people.

There was even sudden movement in an area which, until then, had always proven to be extremely complex and yielded few results: West German–East German relations. Although Honecker had first referred to West Germany as a foreign coun-

try in 1972, and the new, revised constitution no longer spoke of a reunification of the two states, in practice the relationship on both sides was marred by tension. Various deals were made and the details of a common existence were regulated.

The Grundvertrag (Basic Treaty) was of particular significance, and was signed in 1972. It called for good-neighbourly relations from both sides, as well as assurance that violence would never be used. The validity of the existing border should also, in principle, be recognised. However, this did not mean that West Germany recognised the GDR as an international sovereign state. On the contrary, the Reunification Clause in the West German constitution was still valid and it was expressly noted in the Basic Treaty that the border could be altered, should mutual agreements be reached by both sides. This visible expression which changed the situation and eased tensions provided the framework for diplomatic representation known as "Ständige Vertretung" in both states. These were opened in May 1974 in both countries. Since the establishment of embassies would have effectively meant one side's diplomatic recognition of the other (something which the SED leaders deeply desired, but which West Germany categorically rejected), the two countries agreed on this solution which was less binding under international law. From then on, the "Ständige Vertretungen" served as the most important inter-German line of communication. In East Berlin, however, it was to be a source of irritation. Time after time, East German citizens, who saw

^ *Twice a year, the Leipzig Trade Fare exhibits GDR economical progress. The city even exudes international flair.*

no other way out, would flee to the West German diplomatic representation in East Berlin and demand their exit from East Germany. This would continue until 1989.

The GDR seemed to be catching up, becoming more established, and its political leadership considered the country to be on par with West Germany. Honecker and his leading comrades were well and truly convinced that socialism would ultimately prevail—and in their view, this moment was drawing ever closer. If there was ever a concrete piece of evidence needed to highlight this assertion, it manifested itself on 22 June 1974. Something happened which nobody had ever thought possible: on West German soil, of all places, in Hamburg, the GDR's national football team beat the West German team 1-0. It was the only World Cup tournament that the East German team ever qualified for and it beat its official enemy brother. The euphoria that followed was felt even in the highest of political circles. But, as is often the case, the feeling of elation was short-lived. While, despite their historic victory, the GDR team was sent home in the intermediate round, West Germany ultimately went on to win the World Cup. To cap it all off, the victory scorer, Jürgen Sparwasser, fled to West Germany a few years later. It was symbolically apparent: short-term and tightly restricted successes are by no means sufficient to bring about long term stability. Despite its undeniable developments, in terms of its progression it was clear that the GDR was lagging

^ *Hamburg, 22 June 1974. Franz Beckenbauer, Berti Voigts and Martin Hoffmann during the most significant win for the GDR national team.*

behind West Germany: something that would never change.

A further contribution to international recognition for the GDR was its active participation in the Conference on Security and Cooperation in Europe (CSCE). Between 1973 and 1975, important countries from the East and the West took part in the proceedings. The aims included binding agreements in regards to cooperation between both sides of the Iron Curtain, solutions to avoid violence in case disagreements arose, and the implementation of universal human rights regulations. The latter aim proved to be especially problematic for SED rulers. By signing the final act of the Helsinki Agreement on 1 August 1975, they committed themselves to expressly adhering to the compliances surrounding human rights. However, since the final act was not a binding contract under international law, but merely a declaration of intent, those in power in East Berlin did not have to worry about potential consequences if they infringed upon people's fundamental rights. They had, however, underestimated something: from then on, dismayed GDR citizens referred to the contract and demanded that the government adhered to it. In particular, they referred to freedom of movement and the right of abode. As far as domestic policy was concerned, the CSCE had become a political boomerang: who ever wanted to leave East Germany could refer to the signatures on the Helsinki Agreement. Doing so rarely brought about concrete consequences, but did contribute to exposing the morals of the seemingly democratic set-up.

So, the GDR was definitely not as liberal and forward-looking as it had tried to present itself on the world stage. Honecker had clearly not thought about granting "his" people more personal freedom. Elections continued to be nothing but farces in which the political stability (in particular that of the ruling SED) was certain. Where necessary, the party ruled all important parts of each and everyone's life: property, occupational

^ *53 time GDR player, celebrated winner and ultimately vilified as a traitor by the SED: Jürgen Sparwasser.*

outlook, career. Any opinion that diverged too much from the designated path continued to be suppressed. Anyone who was seen to be overtly opposed to the SED still faced the threat of repression and prison. Domestically, talk of class struggle was still rife and since the constitution amendment in 1974, the GDR was now conclusively considered a "socialist state of workers and farmers", which, furthermore, was inseparable from the Soviet Union. For those who submitted themselves to the official rules, or at least resigned to them, it was possible to lead a comfortable life in the early-1970s. Those who did not had to reckon with the tyranny of the state. Below is an excerpt from the diary of a soldier carrying out non-military work after refusing work in the armed forces. The excerpt outlines his superior's reaction:

> "Such sentimentality like that allowed over here would have been impossible under Stalin. Stalin had it right, said the sergeant. We should take our machine guns and kill them or chase them across the mine field."[25]

Stalin's ghost had not been laid to rest, but still hovered over the country and reared its head in political negotiations. Blatant terror was no longer suitable, yet the merciless combat of all real and alleged enemies was still very much on the agenda.

25 Diary entry without date, in: RHG/MG 01 (unnumbered pages).

^ *Federal Chancellor Helmut Schmidt and Erich Honecker sign the Helsinki Final Act, the effects of which were hardly felt.*

This was summed up by the Stasi's infamous directive "1/76" which was put into force on 1 January 1976. Erich Mielke, head of the Stasi, had signed it and, in the best officialese, the following was outlined:

> "The goal of *Zersetzung* is the fragmentation, paralysis, disorganization, and isolation of the hostile and negative forces, in order to impede thereby, in a preventive manner, the hostile and negative doings, to limit them in large part, or to totally avert them, and if applicable to prepare grounds for a political and ideological reestablishment."[26]

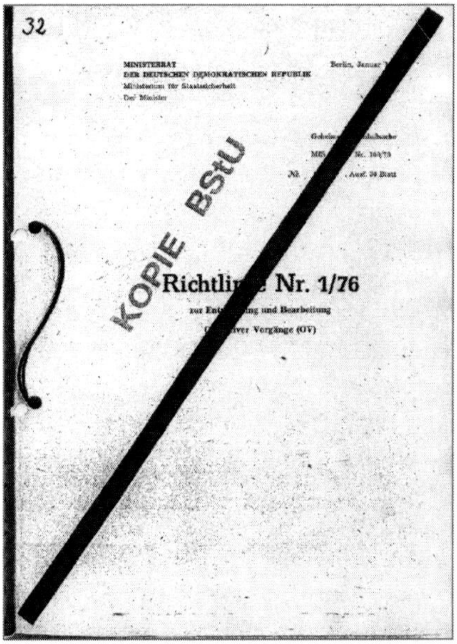

This basically meant that those opposed to the existing political order should be found *before* they became active and that any, truly any, method was permitted in dealing with them. The directive gives a detailed list of what is meant by this, the means allowed included discrediting a person's public reputation by spreading rumours and half-truths, setting up professional and private failures, undermining self-confidence, assigning employment which was far away, and much more. In a country where freedom of press did not exist, where there was no independent judiciary to turn to when faced with such treatment, destroying someone's existence was all too easy. That was the aim and even more tragically, it happened all too often. The SED relentlessly claimed to be the only legitimate people's activists.

26 Ministerium für Staatssicherheit (Ed.): Wörterbuch zur politisch-operativen Arbeit, second edition (1985), keyword: "Zersetzung", GVS JHS 001-400/81, p. 464.

^ *Front page of the infamous "measures of* Zersetzung*". The regime's inhumane face was revealed inside.*

However, this claim could only be deemed valid as long as the people remained silent and did not entertain doubts. If doubts were entertained, the dictatorship immediately reared its ugly head. At this time, it still had the power to do so.

For the time being, however, things remained largely calm in Honecker's state. This was an intrinsic consequence of both the implementation of the "main task", and also of the rise in prosperity. The fact that a great deal was still to be achieved became clear in the mid-1970s. The national economy appeared to be increasingly unable to cope. The increase in productivity, which had been hoped for as a result of the people's increasing loyalty to the state, never happened. It was obvious that the workers and farmers wanted to engage in, and reap, the benefits of the "unity of economic and social policy". That, however, still did not mean they identified with the SED. It certainly did not mean that they would actively get involved with its aims. The retreat back to the supposed non-political niches had begun a long time ago and it would continue to do so at an even faster rate in the coming years. Disillusionment was spreading again.

The SED further contributed to this by continuing to rely on ideological principles when considering economic policies, and when in doubt it dismissed the reality of the circumstances. An example of this was the extreme consolidation processes that were introduced in industry and agriculture. They were so oversized that they were almost impossible to manage and often made losses. However, such phenomena were never addressed, since the official party line was untouchable. Anyone who rebelled against the status quo–albeit on the basis of economic expertise–would have to reckon with being villainised as an opponent and being treated accordingly. This was also something that hindered the people's dedication and intensified their resignation. When the global oil crisis drew near and the Soviet Union announced in 1975 that it could no longer deliver oil to the GDR at subsidised prices, the notion that things were on the up was quashed once and for all. The range of goods on offer in shops deteriorated noticeably, residential construction came to a stand still, there was a nationwide lack of service parts and consumer goods, and it was not forseeable how a stop could be put to this trend.

Inevitably, many people were reminded of the period in which the Wall had been built–not even 15 years ago. Back then, they had been told that things could only get better, but that had only happened within limits. Those who were a little older could still remember the promises made in 1953 and 1958, after the people's uprising and the fifth party conference. The promises had always been big and the people had always been disappointed. The SED continued to claim it was smoothing out the way to a promising future, but ever fewer GDR citizens wanted to believe that. The same old slogans were too hollow and the standard of living did not correspond to the official representation.

Furthermore, a new generation had grown up. This generation had only ever known the GDR and was at a loose end with its heroic founding myths. The momentum from the founding years had long gone and the constant bombardment of anti-fascist legends had steadily lost its effect. The early 1970s had been a period of great awakening and hope, and the disenchantment had been even greater. Once again, the giant leap into socialist utopia had not been achieved. How long were the people going to have to wait? How many more tries would they have to accept? In a world where the media was reaching out to ever more people, it was easy to make a direct comparison with West Germany. Indeed, the GDR was closed off to the

^ *The East German Palace of the Republic was opened in April 1976. It is a venue for both rock concerts and SED party conferences.*

West, but every night on West German television there was an alternative to the dreariness of the SED state. In the previous years, all signs had pointed towards alleviation of tension between the two states, but now there was another factor to take into account: increasing numbers of GDR citizens began to set their living standard against that in West Germany. In comparison, the "Workers' and Peasants' State" came off worse.

^ *Event venue and ceremonial site at the same time. The palace is elegant on the inside – unlike the rest of the GDR.*

WOLF BIERMANN'S EXPATRIATION

The GDR prided itself on being the more humane of the two German states, one that was based on "wholesome" cultural traditions, and one in which there was no place for civil decadence. As was the case in all other important areas, culture was also subject to central control. It was kept in clearly defined boundaries and, ultimately, had to pay homage to socialism. There was scope for freedom, but very little. Anyone who wanted to perform on stage in public and earn a living by doing so had to apply for a permit which could be revoked at any time. The only authority allowed to issue such a permit was the SED.

Being controlled in such a way, it came as surprise to few that the cultural sector in the early 1970s had the same fate seen in other spheres of society. After the "11th Plenum" and its consequences in 1965, there had been no change in cultural policy. Since Honecker's ascent to power, it seemed as though that might change. He went as far as to say that taboos no longer had a place in art now that socialism was established. Suddenly, everything was possible which had previously been ruled out. Critical plays including "The new Sorrows of Young W." by Ulrich Plenzdorf were premiered and were well received by audiences. It was announced that dance music was officially socially acceptable, Rock 'n' Roll, however, (and other varieties) were still frowned upon. "The Legend of Paul and Paula" arrived in cinemas in 1973. It documented everyday life with undertones of scepticism and would influence an entire generation. There was a spirit of optimism in the air again.

That was to come to an abrupt end. In the mid-1970s, when the SED leaders realised that they were about to reach a (economically) political impasse, they feared losing control. At that time, there was no other social area in which such a degree of openness, critical analysis and assertiveness was being displayed as in art and culture. Moreover, the debates that were linked to this did not just take place in closed circles, but all over the country. This prevailed over the state monopoly and, for this reason, the SED leaders decided to take drastic measures.

Individual artists soon saw the adverse effects of criticism under this regime. In 1976, Reiner Kunze was expelled from the East German Association of Writers (DSV) on dubious grounds. He was then target and blanketed by the Stasi. One year later, unnerved, he moved over to West Germany. The popular band "Klaus Renft Combo" was already banned in 1975 and some of its members were arrested. They also found their poise again in West Germany. Films were banned, theatrical productions were prohibited, bans from appearing on stage were issued and cultural establishments were closed down. Those who played along could hope for the party's blessing and with it a career, fame and money. Those who did not play along were considered opponents of the socialist order and were treated as such. That was a harsh reminder of what had gone on in the mid-1960s; it seemed that art and culture had not moved forward in the political system since then. The frustration was even greater when Honecker promised exactly the opposite after coming to power. Increasing numbers of artists left, deeply resigned, to West Germany.

There was one man, however, who did not leave–at least not long-term: Wolf Biermann. The singer-songwriter was a dazzling figure within the East German cultural scene and he already boasted a colourful résumé. Born in 1936 in Hamburg, Biermann grew up in a communist household, his father had been murdered in Auschwitz by the National Socialists. In 1953, at the age of 17, he moved to the GDR due to his communist convictions. In the GDR, he saw the better of the two German states in which his communist ideals would become reality. It was not long before his eyes were opened and he saw the depressing situation there. He was not afraid to talk and

sing about it. In doing so, however, he came into conflict with those in power who had intermittently curry favoured him and offered him chances to further his career. There were many disputes over the years which led to numerous bans from appearing on stage, some of which were administered with great bitterness. Biermann's West German origin and his increasing fame offered a certain amount of protection during these disputes. They could not, however, prevent him from being targeted and monitored by the Stasi. Indeed, in contrast to other GDR citizens, he was permitted to repeatedly travel to West Germany and play there, but from 1965 he was subject to a complete ban from appearing on stage and publishing work in the GDR. Nevertheless, Biermann remained a devout communist and even refused to do the one thing that so many others wanted to do: leave the GDR. This is how he came to be a permanent annoyance to the SED.

The events at a time of intensified cultural politics in November 1976 offered the perfect opportunity to get rid of this

^ *Biermann is allowed to perform his songs to an eager audience at the Academy of Arts in December 1962. He receives a great applause.*

trouble maker. Plans for doing so had already been in the making for years. The SED and the Stasi had worked on many scenarios which could lead to his expatriation, but they wanted to avoid a public dispute with the strident singer. The fact they wanted to avoid such a dispute saved Biermann from a political trial, but helped bring another plan to fruition. When Biermann received an invitation to an event in West Germany, held by the Industrial Union of Metalworkers (IG Metall), he was given permission to leave. The powers that granted permission for him to leave knew that he would not be allowed to return. On the evening of 13 November 1976, Biermann held a concert

for thousands of people. The concert, in Cologne, went on for over four hours and was broadcast live on West German television. The singer did not hold back when criticising the state of affairs in the GDR. He did, however, defend the GDR's right to exist and, on the whole, was keen to defend communism. He received a roaring applause at the end of the evening.

Three days later, on 16 November, the SED Politburo met for its weekly meeting and, in compliance with the plans already made, decided to deny Biermann his return to the GDR. Honecker himself formally proposed this course of action. On 17 November, the rest of the GDR population learned of the news that the singer was being deprived of his GDR citizenship for "gross violation of civic duties". It was further reported that he had brought it on himself with his performance that had been "hostile" towards the GDR[27].

It was by no means the first time that those in power had resorted to this drastic measure to get rid of critical voices. Apparently, expatriation was deemed the most elegant of all possible methods to rid themselves of Biermann. Honecker and his comrades, however, underestimated the explosive nature of the case. As a direct result of the harsh shift in cultural policy which set the frameworks, there was a sudden resistance. In Biermann, a sceptical, but self-professed communist had been expatriated. With such measures being taken, what could people expect in the future? No artist could be sure that their position was secure; it was a fundamental issue. Something that had previously been unimaginable subsequently

27 Neues Deutschland, 17 November 1976, p. 2.

happened: on 17 November, a group of nine prominent artists (eight of which were SED party members) drafted a resolution in protest. In terms of its tone and content, it was extremely reserved. It merely asked that the actions taken be rethought. Among the first to sign were Stefan Heym, Heiner Müller and Christa Wolf. In the days that followed, more than 100 actors, writers, musicians and other, for the most part, well-known artists joined in and added their signatures to the resolution. Since the GDR press was hesitant to print it, the resolution was spread via the West German press. It was an enormous event. There had always been resistance to the SED's dictatorial behaviour and it had been seen in many forms. However, the fact that voices were raised collectively, and not only that, but also from famous GDR citizens who had also profited from the system, gave a new quality to the resistence.

The SED was preparing to counteract. Since it was almost impossible to discipline all the artists directly without further collateral damage, a new defamation campaign began. The media–which had been brought into line by the SED–printed scores of declarations in approval of decisions made by the SED. Alongside the unknown "workers", there were also statements from popular colleagues of those attacked including Anna Seghers, Ludwig Renn and Berlin's cabaret theatre "Die Distel". Public events were organised which aimed to have the same effect as the statements. The GDR's artistic community

^ *Cologne, November 1976. Biermann at what is probably his most important concert. Hours of singing, discussion and intent listening.*

was deeply divided and opportunists began to make an appearance. They sought personal gain by surrendering and condemning the resolutions. The conflict became more and more heated, pressure on the signatories increased and eventually the party imposed scores of punishments. Many were excluded from their professional associations and performances were restricted. As a result, some withdrew their signatures, but there was a more significant consequence: many of those involved left the GDR and moved over to West Germany. The SED leaders were only too pleased to let them leave and granted their exit, for the most part, without hindrance, as this would reduce the risk of unrest among the citizens of the GDR. The GDR would never recover from losing these artists.

The conflict surrounding Wolf Biermann, however, ran much deeper. Once again, the SED had shown its true, ugly face. Whenever its power was in question, the SED did not hesitate to defend itself with the most brutal of measures. This had always been the case and the "Biermann case" went to show that nothing had changed. Honecker's attempt to present himself as an open-minded, even liberal father for the country had failed for good. His "unity of economic and social policy" had to be seen as failing–not least due to the debts that were spiralling out of control. The people increasingly lost their belief in success for the socialist GDR. But that certainly did not mean that the country's destiny had already been decided. However, it was clear that the chances of survival would de-

^ *As well as protests from prominent GDR artists, there are also countless, mostly anonymous, protests from the people.*

crease unless fundamental changes to the political, economical and social system were made. But where would the will to change come from? This question had to be asked in light of the circumstances surrounding Biermann's expatriation. It was evident that Honecker and the leaders of the SED were not prepared for change.

Even Biermann recognised and addressed the irony of his expatriation. In his song entitled "Populär-Ballade", he wrote: "You're putting out the fire with fuel, you won't put the fire out anymore." and further, "You're doing what you wanted to prevent, you're making me famous". Indeed, he had been famous until November 1976, but for the majority of GDR citizens he was of no significance. That all changed when he was expatriated. His expatriation meant more than getting rid of an unpopular singer. Fundamental shortfalls in the "Workers' and Peasants' State" had been revealed, shortfalls which would ultimately lead to its downfall.

^ *Biermann also enjoys support in West Germany. Among others, such support comes from Günter Wallraff and Rudi Dutschke.*

7 SEPTEMBER 1987

A VISIT TO WEST GERMANY

ON THE BRINK OF THE LAST DECADE

In the late 1970s, disillusionment came to pass once and for all in the GDR. The people no longer expected any significant improvement to the situation and the SED leadership knew that its "unity of economic and social policy" was failing. The Soviet Union, increasingly concerned with its own economic problems, no longer considered itself in the position to support its East German placeholder to the same extent it had until then. The acceleration of the arms race meant the protecting power was in even more difficulties from 1978. The problems worsened a year later when the Soviet Union invaded Afghanistan. In December 1981, the Polish government reacted to democratic aspirations by introducing martial law. This resulted in dramatically fewer imports to the GDR (including much needed primary materials) as well as the need to financially support its neighbour in the East. The "Workers' and Peasants' State" could not actually afford to do this, but those in power were too afraid that the opposition movement would jump over into East Germany. For this reason Poland had to be stabilised, but that meant spending money. Money that was in part from the GDR.

Domestically, the imbalance of concentration on the consumer sector led to signs of deficit in all other areas, as well as to massive business closures and a decline in innovation. The negative effects of the excessive concentration and specialisation of manufacturing cooperatives could be seen in agriculture: agricultural businesses became unprofitable and the division of cattle and crop farming resulted in numerous

complications. A number of bad harvests did not help the situation. People everywhere were living on the breadline. The effects this could have on the individual are highlighted in this handwritten letter of complaint to the GDR's Central Committee from a collective farmer in Angermünde. Admittedly, it is a drastic case, but not uncommon in 1980:

> "I am writing things as I see them. From the outside, my home looks like a stable, the framing of the build-

^ *"As we work today, so shall we live tomorrow", the motto of the day. There is hope, but signs of stagnation are increasing.*

ing can be seen. There is a barn attached to the house. The barn is derelict and if it collapses then so will the house. The doors are falling out of their frames, the furnaces have collapsed, the kitchen cannot be called a kitchen, and there is no water main. I have to fetch water from outside. There are no decent cooking facilities, no toilets. The cellar has collapsed. The agricultural cooperative is responsible for this. I have been visited many times by representatives. They think they can get away

^ *August 1980. Life goes on, the sun shines. Economically, however, the country is on the verge of collapse.*

with it because I am single and bringing up three children who still have to attend school."

Upon inspection by the SED district committee a few weeks later, it was concluded that "all the facts and figures are correct". A few of the smaller problems were dealt with and the promise of a new bathroom and lavatory made for 1981. However, when the time came, the plans had to be moved back again, due to "lack of resources".[28]

It was without a doubt that living conditions for the GDR citizens had dramatically improved over the last few decades. However, expectation and reality were growing further and further apart. While the country was being celebrated on the international stage as one of the ten most significant industrial nations, at home things were hardly moving forward. The infrastructure deteriorated and the gap in technological development between the GDR and the West became even bigger.

The mess the SED leaders found themselves in was a result of the spiralling debt caused by their consumption politics. The money owed to non-socialist foreign countries had increased more than tenfold within a decade, and the country was now hardly able to pay back the interest rates alone. One possibility to break the vicious circle seemed to be loans from the West. They would not be a long-term solution, but they could fill in the holes, at least for the short-term. There were voices that warned against becoming too dependant on the West, in particular West Germany, but there did not seem to be another choice. SED member Günter Schabowski had a further consideration and his words were put on record. Those in power still considered themselves the "imminent victors of history". Ultimately, according to Schabowski, "the superiority of our social system will be proved. And what is so bad about letting capitalism finance it until then?"[29] In hindsight, such comments may appear to be naïve, but this really was at the centre of communist thinking and helps to explain why the leading figures in the SED never thought about fundamental

28 Cf. numerous documents about this case in: Bundesarchiv (BArch), DY 30/1930.

29 Interview with Günter Schabowski, in: Jens Schöne, Stabilität und Niedergang. Ost-Berlin im Jahr 1987, Berlin 2010, here p. 96.

changes despite recognising some problems, and they looked on as their demise ensued.

At the start of the 1980s, the GDR would really go to any lengths in order to get hold of Western money. They sold everything they could, this ranged from valuable produce to political prisoners. Soviet oil, which had been sent for the GDR, was then processed and sold on to West Germany. As a result, there were shortages in the GDR. Waiting times for cars, televisions and telephones continued to increase and so, too, did the frustration. The boiling point was still to come.

^ *Undeterred by the growing problems, the SED moves forward with old methods. There are no solutions to the growing number of problems in sight.*

The GDR was now dependent on Western loans and, internally, politicians had acknowledged that debts of more than 20 billion Deutschmarks could no longer be regulated without external help. There were some frantic suggestions, one was that Moscow should pay off the debts and, in return, the GDR would cease trading with West Germany and only supply the Soviet Union instead. During times of cross-system globalisation, this idea was obviously absurd and Honecker would have to be given a dressing down by Brezhnev. The fact that such thoughts were entertained and communicated highlights just how desperate the situation had become.

The last decade had been hard in both the West and the East, and the oil crisis was a clear manifestation of this. While other market-based democracies had used this downturn as a opportunity for upheaval, for reframing and to change structures, the Eastern block held on to its old views. This prevented any such approach to solutions being made and the "Workers' and Peasants' State" suffered mercilessly.

Lenders had lost their faith in socialist states since Poland had declared itself bankrupt and Romania had requested a line of credit from the International Monetary Fund. In the first six months of 1982 alone, the West withdrew 40 percent of its short-term investments from the GDR and there was no refund in sight. The country was now well and truly in the debt trap. Quite simply, it lacked foreign cash. The overall bad situation escalated and resulted most notably in a widespread supply crisis. This was not just something that had taken place in 1982,

but now it was really felt. Until then, the GDR had lived off ever decreasing materials, and in the following years would be helped by West Germany of all places. 1982, however, was the year in which everything came to a head. Long queues outside shops had always existed, but now they were longer. Empty shelves were part of everyday life by this point, but even the basics were now in short supply. Nobody starved, but the efforts people had to go to in order to secure a decent, balanced and varied diet were great. People bought things when they were there, no matter what they were. The fact this often took place during work hours did little to alleviate the situation, but was tolerated in (most) cases since everyone had the same problem.

There was panic within the government due to the desolate situation which continued to worsen. In February, there had been talk of "supply gaps" and "considerable decrease in quality" in certain foods. By midyear, those in power were busy trying to fill the gaps any way they could. Tonnes of bulbs from state seed potato supplies were released for consumption. The amount of meat in sausage was also to sink. Attempts to make stocks go further by adding bread to liver sausages and black pudding were met with refusal from the people. New kinds of margarine and butter came onto the market and all of them had one thing in common: they all contained less fat than

^ *What will later ironically be called the "socialist waiting community" is, in 1982, a harsh reality: queuing for hours.*

the previous kinds. The industrial sector also suffered due to the lack of animal and vegetable fat. Even the process used to make bird food was changed according to central orders; it was now only to contain domestic products. Emergency plans were even made which would come into effect in the event of GDR having to stop imports of foreign grain. Even when there was good news, it was often overshadowed by predicaments in other places. For example, the SED Central Committee enjoyed a great harvest of soft fruit at the end of July 1982, but there was a shortage of sugar needed to preserve the fruit.

There was another, very basic problem that was related not only to the shortage in oil, but also to the growing backlog of modernisation. There was a lack of public transport and logistical facilities throughout the country. Transport still worked in rural areas, but that was mainly due to the gallant efforts of the people living there. There were local transport connections, but fewer and fewer national connections were running. For this reason, the Ministry for Transport submitted concrete plans to reopen 186 stations that had been closed down. But these plans also failed due to the lack of funds that would have been needed.

This was all in stark contrast to developments in West Germany, and that did not go unnoticed. 1982 was not an econom-

^ *Enormous queues even form in front of bookshops – even in the capital city which is always the first to be supplied.*

ically successful year for West Germany either, but things appeared to work a lot better. Millions of GDR citizens convinced themselves of this every evening as they tuned in to West German television, escaping the East via television. The connection with their own country continued to get even weaker. This phenomenon was aggravated by the SED demanding new and extensive expressions of loyalty from the people. In March 1982, a new law came into effect. It was then that the firing order was first established. Despite having signed the final report at the Conference on Security and Cooperation in Europe, which stipulated that everyone had the right to choose their place of abode, those in power now formally obligated their soldiers to shoot at "criminals" who tried to escape over the border. Under certain conditions, a new National Service Act now allowed women to join the army, and anyone who evaded (by now compulsory) "socialist military education", lost their right to an apprenticeship place. They could also be demoted in the work place and only employed as unskilled labourers.

Something commonly found on jackets and bags in 1982 was the "Swords to Ploughshares" symbol: a blacksmith transforming a sword. The symbol was used by oppositionists of the worldwide arms race. The SED reacted with a number of disciplinary actions, they feared the negative effects on its own

^ *A much loved way of escaping the dreariness of the GDR: watching West German TV, seen here in Lichtenhagen, Rostock.*

militarisation plans, in particular among the younger people in the country. To this end, the SED tried to get the church on its side. Speaking on behalf of the church, regional bishop Johannes Hempel straightforwardly noted that it could have no influence. In March 1982, Hempel warned against further aggressive moves. He said such moves were "more likely to worsen the situation than to discourage young people." He also gave a warning which had a fey-like tone to it:

> "He was concerned that any harsh government reaction towards the youngsters would exacerbate the trend among those teenagers who did not have any kind of religious motivation at all, to find a place for their political opposition in the church."[30]

His warning to the SED, to make use of its time and not to provoke self-inflicted opposition against its own politics, was ignored. Seven years later, when resignation turned to decisive action, this would take on a significant role. The main contradiction of 1982 was all too clear: the SED, after three decades in power, was not able to adequately feed its people. Never

30 Information about State Secretary Klaus Gysi's conversation with regional bishop Hempel on 12.3.1982 (sgd. Gysi), in: StAufarb., Rainer Eppelmann, no. 260.

^ *Karl-Eduard von Schnitzler, nicknamed* Sudel-Ede *(sully Eddy). His weekly show "The Black Channel" was very anti-West Germany.*

before had there been such a dilemma and never before had reality and the image portrayed in the controlled media been further apart from each other. The mood that resulted is best summed up by a technologist from Premnitz in Brandenburg on the last working day of the year: "And then the question: what is black and just around the corner? Everyone knew it and they all agreed: the New Year. Sobering. So, here's to 1983."[31]

31 Jeannette Madarász-Lebenhagen (Ed.), Alltag im ostdeutschen Premnitz. Mit den Kalenderblättern (1982-1984) von Hubert Biebl, Berlin 2012, p. 29.

^ *1982, deadly silence at the Brandenburg Gate. All desires for change die away, alternative ideas are rigorously criminalised.*

INTERIOR EROSION

The truly dramatic situation in the GDR subsided again in 1983, above all due to a loan worth billions. The West German government acted as a guarantor and poured piles of money into the "Workers' and Peasants' State". Of all places, it was the other German state that rescued the GDR. A deciding factor for doing so was fear from Bonn and Munich that instability in the GDR could lead to instability throughout Europe. The consequences of this would be unimaginable and, during the tense times of the arms race, would almost certainly lead to military conflict. This was to be prevented at all costs. The loans, worth billions, in 1983 and 1984 were the price that had to be paid and the West German government was willing to pay.

Materialistically, the situation in the GDR improved quickly, but the catastrophic circumstances from 1982 left traces. Much of the population had already lost faith in the socialist utopia. Behind closed doors, people liked to (quite rightly) complain about the situation. Those in power could not rely on loyalty anymore. Long before its core had been cut out, more and more people detached themselves from the SED and its publicised goals – this would later be considered opposition in terms of the GDR's history. There was also another new factor: the uncertainty, right through to the rejection of the party line, now reached the country's functional elite who were supposed to be responsible for implementing the rules and ensuring stability.

All of a sudden, the Stasi was coming across the same phenomenon all over the country. "Destructive" behaviour, "panic

mongering" and "moaning" was spreading among the leading economical cadre, who, in most cases, were also members of the SED. There was great unrest among the cadres as they could not communicate the massive range of problems faced by the workers any more. The "political and ideological basic position of a large proportion of the cadres" had supposedly already been negative at the start of the catastrophic year of 1982. Some of them had "inbuilt problems and contradictions and would therefore see our social situation as insoluble."[32] That was a clear rejection of the actual socialist conditions in the GDR and it had been made by officials who often had the "Workers' and Peasants' State" to thank. If they themselves did not consider it possible to solve the problems within the SED dictatorship, then that could not be without consequence in the long term.

For now, however, it remained calm, despite the advancing disillusionment. Those responsible carried on with their work and, for the most part, tried to complete it to the best of their ability with the means available. Their loyalty, on the other hand, had suffered and in trying times they would probably not jump to defend the system. The outright protest that followed could not have been foreseen, but faith in the socialist future had been destroyed. The interior erosion of the GDR advanced.

32 Leiterinformation 1/82 from 28 January 1982, in: BStU, BV Potsdam, AKG 1318, Bl. 5f.

^ *Controversial friendship. Franz Josef Strauß and Alexander Schalck-Golodkowski lead secret negotiations for the billion-Deutschmark loans.*

While functionaries and the people were going through a process of disillusionment, a small minority began to take action against the current state of things. Since there was no parliamentary opposition (or any other kind), but just that which had been simulated by bloc parties, any kind of digression from the party line was a punishable offence. Cautious, non conformative behaviour did, however, begin to develop. Opposition to the system had always existed, it ranged from resolute anti-communism to communist reformers. Opponents attacked the political system, sometimes directly, in the early years of the "Workers' and Peasants' State" to put an end to it, but this was different now. By now, a new generation had grown up. Brought up in the GDR, this generation had no concept of a unified Germany. For this reason, their revolt did not really aim for reunification of the two German states, but for changes to the current state of affairs. Reform, not revolution was their aim. Anything else would have been self-destructive as the dictatorship had no tolerance for any kind of divergent behaviour. Slowly, carefully and taking small steps, a civil countermovement began to develop, one which was never made up of more than a small minority of the population. Nevertheless, it would become of great significance at the end of the 1980s.

It was under church protection where opposition was most widely manifest. The relationship between the SED state and religious bodies had been through many phases. This was especially true for the Evangelical Church and, at times, there had been bitter conflicts between the two. By now, however, relations between the two were good. The self-proclaimed "party of the working classes" still, however, considered religion to be like opium for the people, as backward and antiquated. Having close ties to the church and being open about it could still be detrimental to one's career. Only those who were open about their faith in socialism could hope for the blessing of the state.

In all other respects, the church was an autonomous institution within the GDR, and was tolerated by those in power. It maintained its own educational institutions, published its own works and, at least internally, had a pluralistic approach to freedom of expression.

For those reasons, it became more interesting to those people in the dictatorship who felt constrained, who wanted to ex-

press their opinions and who cherished alternative ideas to the dull reality. People did not have to be religious to seek out a church. Increasing numbers of people attended church as they were generally dissatisfied with their personal circumstances. People got to know new people, they socialised and began to create a network for the first time.

Bishop Hempel's fear that the SED could create oppositional powers with its uncompromising methods cannot be denied. Opposition often began with small, rather unpolitical expressions or actions. Similar to West Germany, peace and the environment were also central issues. They were increasingly followed by the question of human rights. Any activity that digressed from the party line was systematically criminalised by the SED.

^ *Oppositional ideas and protests are not completely out of sight, like here in May 1983 in Jena.*

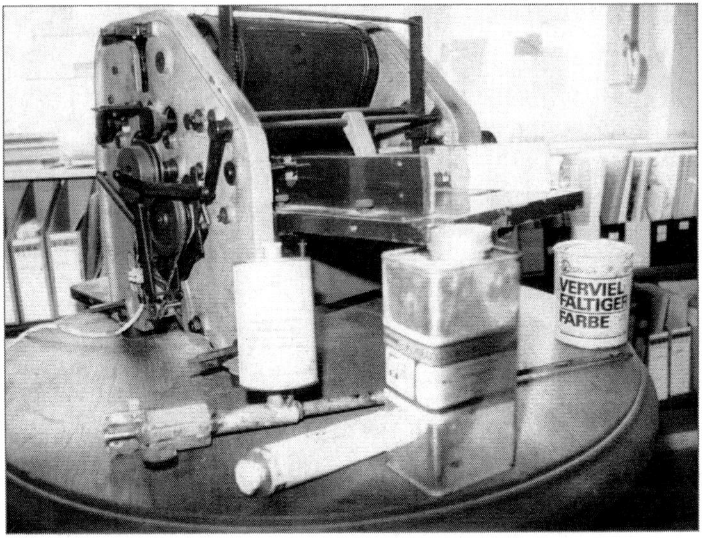

If a person was to find fault with environmental damage that had been caused by the worn out economy, the Stasi could be very quick to get involved, as was the case in 1985 in a small town called Retzow in Brandenburg. Groundwater here had been contaminated for years by sewage and dumping from the local producers' cooperative. Despite repeated complaints, nothing had changed and those responsible only went about acting when their own positions were in danger: "Since the problem has not been solved in the last few years, the government loses its credibility in securing environmental protection." Even worse: "Due to the most recent actions of the protestant church in the area of ecology, there is a chance of spreading this problem via the connected congregations in question."[33] A frenzy broke out. On the one hand, actions were actually going to be taken to improve the situation. (This, however, would never actually happen, also due to the general lack of available resources.) On the other hand, the Stasi initiated an extensive investigation which concentrated on the local vicar and other local people. They were now under the observation of the secret police and under suspicion of harbouring oppositional thoughts and ideas: an altogether typical event for

33 Information from 20.5.1985, in: BStU, BV Potsdam, AKG 744, Bl. 269f.

^ *Illegal publications increase, pointing out what is wrong with the system. Getting hold of the right equipment is difficult.*

the GDR in the 1980s. On the whole, the country seemed to be quite stable at this point in time, under the surface, however, things were shaking. At first, neither the pervasive resignation, nor the emerging opposition represented a threat to the SED's existence. It would be a mistake to claim that the way forward had already been sketched out with no alternative. There was still the time and the opportunity to resist, to stop the interior erosion and consolidate the political system. Nobody could have known that the party would also prove itself not to be in the position in the future. On the contrary, just a few years before the end of the "Workers' and Peasants' State", its general secretary was heading for his biggest political triumph: Erich Honecker made an official visit to West Germany which he had vilified so much.

^ *Printing paper is also in short supply. The Stasi intensely observes and documents any suspicious activity.*

^ *Whitsun 1987. Young people protest in East Berlin; their calls are loud: "The Wall has to go". The police take decisive action.*

ERICH HONECKER IN BONN

In the 1980s, East-West German summit meetings took place mainly in Moscow. After the West German federal chancellor Helmut Schmidt had made a working visit to the GDR in December 1981, he was then seen again in the Soviet Union. The reason for his visit was as simple as it was morbid: between 1982 and 1985, three CPSU general secretaries had died. Politicians from allover the world travelled to be at their funerals. It was here that Honecker and Helmut Kohl met, Kohl had taken office in 1982 and he renewed an invitation to West Berlin which had been given before by Schmidt.

The arms race and the confrontation between the power blocks that came with it had had a positive effect on intra-German relations in the past few years. They were never conflict-free, but they were both of the conviction that normalisation would be beneficial to both sides. The GDR was aiming for further recognition of its existence and economical benefits, and West Germany was aiming for a gradual, evolutionary change to the "Workers' and Peasants' State". What appeared to be a joint convergence between the two negotiating partners, was watched closely by the Soviet Union. As had always been the case, the GDR did not have all the power, the power of veto remained in Moscow. This was used in 1984 when the first meeting between Honecker and Kohl was due to take place on West German soil. It was Mikhail Gorbachev, who would later rise to become the bearer of hope, who was given the job of stopping the meeting which had already been planned. Honecker, on the brink of his most politically significant coup,

had to cancel the trip on very flimsy grounds. After Gorbachev had won new leeway by being elected Soviet leader in March 1985, no more obstacles were put in the way, and plans for a meeting could be made.

For Honecker and the politics he represented, there were many reasons that made the meeting seem so attractive. A visit in Bonn would make it appear to the rest of the world as though the GDR was on the same level as West Germany, the first secretary would demonstrate strength in foreign politics and it would give the impression that he had all the power in his country–which was not at all true. West Germany had never recognised the "Workers' and Peasants' State", its constitution was based on the Reunification Clause - however, Honecker was about to walk along the red carpet in the West German capital with the chancellor. Inwardly, that was an important signal: the more the loyalty dwindled among its own people, the more important it was for the SED to exhibit success in other areas. There had been more illusion than reality in the GDR, and for that reason such intense pictures were even more important: "The reception in Bonn in September 1987 was friendly. The national anthem was heard for the first time in Bonn and the state's flag raised."[34]

34 Erich Honecker, Moabiter Notizen. Berlin 1994, p. 47.

^ *The new leader from Moscow: Mikhail Gorbachev. Due to his reforms, he is not as popular as his predecessor.*

The importance SED leaders attached to the occasion can be seen in their actions before the meeting. Great efforts were made to make it appear as though the SED was a humane party that treated its people with tolerance and leniency. In July 1987, the head-of-state-council of the GDR abolished the death penalty and a general amnesty was granted which saw more than 24,000 convicts released from prison. In 1987, there was "only" one death at the Berlin Wall – that was a quarter of the number seen in the previous year. This one death, however, proved that nothing had changed principally. The SED leaders only thought about changing the appearance of the party, and not about changing their basic approach to reform the dictatorship. The SED leaders, and only the SED leaders, were in power and they would go to any length to defend it. Nothing had changed in respect to this in the last few decades. Only unconditional compliance with socialism guaranteed personal prosperity. Anyone who even tried to escape had to reckon with drastic consequences.

While Honecker made preparations for his visit to the West, the borders to it remained sealed. Everyday GDR citizens still had to hand in a reasoned application if they wanted to cross the deadly border. The application would then be approved (or not) by the SED administration. The criteria for this decision were not clear and appeals were not allowed. This was a dictatorship and everyone had to bow down to it. Daily

^ *A ceremonial, but chilly welcome from Federal Chancellor Kohl. The first time a GDR head of state visits West Germany.*

reports in the GDR's media claimed the party was doing everything for the good of the people. Internally, however, the talk was much more to the point. For example, in January 1987, a high-ranking member of the Stasi told leading members of the police that it was "not at all" the party's intention that "as many GDR citizens could travel, but above all the right kind of citizens". The right kind of citizen was defined by the party and not by the "beliefs and demands of the people".[35]

Ahead of Honecker's visit to Bonn, the GDR was celebrating itself as a modern, liberal and visionary state while the opposite was in fact the case. This ploy was, however, success-

ful and parts of the Western world fell for it. The country considered itself to be a giant and there were few who could see that the country was built on a crumbling pedestal. With his chest literally swelling with pride, Honecker travelled to West Germany. The trip would also have an emotional climax when Honecker would visit his sister and the house where he was born in the Saarland.

The visit, which took place between 7 and 11 September, was officially a working visit, but Honecker was welcomed with all the honour and protocol normally given to a head of state. The itinerary was extensive: he had talks with West German President Richard von Weizsäcker, Bavarian Minister-President Franz Josef Strauß and his counterpart from the Saarland Oskar Lafontaine. Honecker held talks in the Krupp family's ancestral home Villa Hügel, as well as with leading economical representatives. He also paid a nostalgic visit to Herbert Wehner, a childhood friend and former member of the Communist Party who joined the Social Democrats (SPD) after World War II, and who was now seriously ill. More than 2,000 journalists sent live reports and produced much sought after pictures and texts. It appeared as though Honecker was at the height of his power: a statesman watched by the world, rubbing shoulders with the big Western names who were all too happy to welcome him. That was also a sign to Moscow. Gorbachev had just begun to carefully implement his policies of glasnost and perestroika–openness and reconstruction–policies which the SED distanced itself from. In doing

35 Speech by major general Büchner, 28 January 1987, in: BStU, HA VII, Nr. 483, Bd. 1, part 1 of 2.

so, Honecker turned away from the longstanding protecting power, forgetting who was to thank for the GDR's existence. This would not remain without consequence.

The public highlight of the intra-German summit was a gala dinner in Bonn on the evening of 7 September 1987. Chancellor Kohl was the host, and the event was broadcast on live television in both German states. The differing views in relation to intra-German policy were never made more clear than they were on this evening. During his toast, Kohl emphasised that, despite the rapprochement, nothing had changed in relation to the contradicting views in principal matters. The need for the two German states to be reunified was made clear in the constitution, this was and would remain the aim of his policy. Honecker had nothing substantial to argue back. With a stern expression and in a squeaky voice, he reminded that the facts should be recognised and the relationship between the two should continue to be normalised. He claimed that the borders throughout Europe should remain and were a condition for peace for which the GDR would continue to fight for, whatever it took. The evening dragged on, but Honecker had made his point: he was sitting there in Bonn and not Gorbachev, he was sat in front of the international press. This seemed to confirm his leadership and destroy some of the doubts. The GDR seemed to have finally found a place in the international community of states.

^ *It is astonishing that it even took place, even more so that it was broadcast live: the gala dinner from 7 September 1987.*

However, not every meeting ran so smoothly. The two German leaders met again on 8 September. The day before, the firing order at the inner-German border and Berlin Wall (which Honecker obviously denied) had been discussed by the innermost SED members in the GDR. Honecker's reaction to Kohl's remarks were very different than they had been the night before: had there not just been an amnesty which meant there were no longer political prisoners in the GDR? Among those released, had there not been individuals "who wished to move to West Germany"? Honecker claimed that such wishes to leave the GDR would be granted "without reservation". If West Germany wanted further talks on reuniting families, this could obviously be considered. Any further requests should be submitted for review. Obviously, there was a desire to approach these problems in a sympathetic manor. Once again, Honecker had created an image of a tolerant, open-minded GDR leadership which was prepared to talk about anything. Of course there were problems, but they could be solved with mutual dialogue.The times of the Cold War seemed to be over between the two states and this had a profound effect on the SED's domestic policy: "There are no prisoners being held for political reasons."[36] Once again, this was not the truth, but it aimed to clarify the stability of the current situation. After all, if all political prisoners were released in one go, then there was no reason for the SED to be afraid of them. That, at least, is the impression that Honecker tried to convey and, to a certain extent, he was successful.

And so, the visit to West Germany was a great success from the Eastern perspective. Indeed, only a few contracts of lesser importance had been signed between the two – covering issues including radiation protection and scientific and engineering cooperation – but this was not the main issue. The ageing leader headed back to the GDR. Nobody could know it at this point, but in little more than two years, he would suffer a humiliating fall from power.

36 Transcript of talks on 7 and 8 September 1987 in Bonn, in: SAPMO-BArch, DY 30/ Büro Honecker, no. 2.397.

^ *State visit concluded, contracts signed and the next party conference just around the corner. The future seems certain. For now.*

BERLIN

^ *A highlight of 1987: Berlin's 750th birthday. The celebrations are pompous and expensive, the debts begin to spiral out of control.*

WINZER

^ *More sights that had by now become the norm in the divided city: walls, watch towers, deathstrip.*

^ *The Wall stretches 47.3 kilometres through Berlin. It has now been standing for 26 years. How much longer?*

9 NOVEMBER 1989
THE FALL OF THE BERLIN WALL

BEFORE THE STORM

Honecker had not long been back in his "Workers' and Peasants' State" before the SED showed its true colours. Now that the important visit in Bonn was over, things could return to how they had been before. It was not long before the repercussions of this were seen. On 17 October 1987, a group of skinheads raided a concert by the band "Element of Crime" in the Zionskirche (Church of Zion). There were neo-Nazi chants and visitors were randomly beaten. Nothing was done to stop it. The omnipresent state powers did not step in to help, despite being present. Apparently it was more important to discipline the group of mainly alternative concertgoers than to act against the right wing extremist behaviour. Fur-

^ *A subculture that transcended borders had long since been established: Element of Crime arrives from West Berlin to perform a concert.*

thermore, according to the SED's definition, this kind of mindset did not exist in the GDR. Since anything that was not part of the ideological plan could not exist, the event was simply ignored. This led to increasing protests which demanded court proceedings against the perpetrators and, ultimately, more severe punishments than had been given out until now. This process had a new quality to it: first of all, the storm of protest was not only made up of opposition groups, but also of everyday people. It also showed that it was possible to budge the government if enough effort was put in. This was an early indication of the significant events that were to take place in 1989.

It was not long before there was another trial of strength on the part of those in power. This time, it would really go after the opposition, and the Zionskirche would be at the centre of the events once more. There, in its cellars, an Umweltbibliothek (Environmental Library) had been set up. Those wishing to read undesired and forbidden texts could get hold of them here. The church rooms and Honecker's visit to Bonn had offered a certain amount of protection, but that was no longer the case by winter 1987. Overnight from 24 to 25 November, members of the Stasi and the state department for public prosecution occupied the library. Those present were arrested and the material found was confiscated. "Aktion Falle", as it was called in Stasi jargon, aimed to criminalise the opposition and prevent it from growing. Exactly the opposite actually happened. There was a wave of solidarity: opposition groups who had previously quarrelled with each other suddenly talked with each other and issued joint statements. Public vigils were held for those who had been arrested, and members of the public, who normally kept their distance from the opposition groups, supplied tea and sandwiches. Bärbel Bohley, an important figure for the Peaceful Revolution in 1989/1990, later recalls:

> "For us, this new kind of involvement was indeed a sign of hope. It showed that we, the 'narrow-gauge opposition', were being taken seriously by the people. These people were obviously observing us to the best of their ability. Even if we didn't consider ourselves opposition-

ists at all. And in 1987 more and more people got involved, took up positions and voiced their opinions."[37]

A process had begun which would later be felt throughout the entire country, and it was by no means limited to East Berlin. Silent resignation was increasingly turning into activism, even if this did at first remain limited to small minorities of the population. The GDR was certainly not in a state of revolutionary unrest, but the signals that something was wrong in Honecker's state were increasing.

Things that had previously seemed unthinkable were happening. More and more demonstrations were taking place and in 1988 they were seen in towns and cities including Bautzen, Erfurt, Leipzig, Pasewalk and Schwerin. The SED leader of a publicly owned business replied when asked how things would develop in the coming years: "Work and living conditions will not improve greatly again until 1995."[38] References to Wolf Biermann were made throughout the GDR, like in the small village of Garlitz (Potsdam). Even the weakest of the weak began to rebel: workers from Mozambique repeatedly went on strike. They had been flown from their home country to help solve the problem of labour shortages and, effectively, they had no rights. They were also now in the position to enforce their, on the whole, warranted wishes as part of the industrial action.

All of these activities took place individually, uncoordinated and, in most cases, were not seen by the majority of the public. They were no way near significant enough to have posed a real danger to those in power. They did, however, make it clear that pressure in domestic policy was increasing, that more and more people were unhappy with their situation and were now prepared to make it public.

This willingness was not least a result of the fact that the overall situation had not improved, but continued to worsen. The range of goods available in shops continued to sink, the queues in front of the shops grew, environmental pollution increased rapidly, the empty propaganda slogans could no longer

37 Interview with Bärbel Bohley, in: Schöne, Stabilität und Niedergang, p. 79.

38 Party leadership statement from 21 November 1988, in: BStU, BV Potsdam, 1. Stellvertreter Operativ, Nr. 7 Bl. 21.

cover up the fact that there was no plan for the future and industrial production was falling to its knees.

A symbol of this–as well as of the complete inability of those in power to react appropriately–is a plea for help that came from Halle in early 1988. The manager at a publicly owned slaughter and processing company had raised the alarm due to the awful working conditions. The inspection that followed showed that the cooling system, which had been in operation there for 53 years, was "very worn out" and "the overall system in need of general repair due to extensive corrosion". The basic problem: the system contained ten tonnes of highly poisonous ammonia. Everyone involved agreed that the company had become "a serious danger to the health and lives of the workers and nearby residential population". It was urgently recommended that it be torn down promptly. But nothing happened. The reason: some leading politicians in East Berlin feared that the supply of meat in some areas of the GDR would drop if the company was to close. Since funds for urgent maintenance were also lacking, another, altogether unsuitable instruction was given: business was to go on as usual and safety would be assured by "controls around the clock".[39] This was nothing less than absurd and demonstrated the huge problems in the GDR shortly before its end. Like this company, the rest of the country trudged along until then on the edge of collapse. This could not be seen on the surface, but looking deeper, the problems were accumulating to an extent which would not be manageable when the situation ultimately escalated.

39 Information about an emergency situation (n.d.), in: SAPMO-BArch, DY 30/203.

"WE ARE THE PEOPLE!"

On the evening of 30 April 1989, public festivals were being held throughout the GDR. Most started with very official torch light processions and ended on local festival grounds. They were all held to mark International Worker's Day on 1 May. This had been the tradition for many years. The rituals were now bereft of meaning, but the people used the day as a reason to join together in celebration. Such occasions were always welcome and alcohol consumption was high in many places. Großwudicke, in Potsdam, was one such place. What happened here was a taste of things to come; the village anticipated the world changing events to come.

The Stasi later noted that it all began with what were generally "Ironic remarks about the mayor". However, things soon took a turn for the worse. A number of members from the volunteer fire department formed a group and began singing at the top of their voices: "40 square metres, minefields, barbed wire, now you know where I live, in the zone". But the singing did not stop there. What followed was a clear declaration to the political system: "Germany will be united, let's pull down the Wall now".[40]

At this point in April 1989, the idea that the Wall could fall still seemed highly unlikely. Few people could have imagined that it would ever fall, and Honecker had recently pointed out that it would still be standing in 50 or 100 years, unless there were fundamental changes. On the whole, the country was still

40 Information from 3 May 1989, in: BStU, BV Potsdam, AKG 399, part 2, Bl. 722.

calm, but that was to change very soon: changes were on the horizon.

The first signs of change were the local elections on 7 May 1989. Voting, in the true sense of the word, had not existed in the GDR for years. Elections were complete farces and the results had been determined in advance by the SED. For this reason, it was no surprise when the media announced that 95.85 percent of voters had voted for the SED and its allies. That would have normally been the end of the matter, but not this time. Representatives of the opposition had put their rights to use and observed the ballot-counting up and down the country. For the first time, there was proof of what everybody already knew: the election results were rigged. There was widespread anger, and complaints were made to the central election commission. The commission refused to process the complaints and by mid-June substantial amounts of documents had already been destroyed. The signal this sent out was clear: the SED was untouchable and nothing about that was going to change.

Around the same time, a rumour was being spread around the GDR: Hungary had opened its border to Austria. For the first time since 1961, there was a gap in the Iron Curtain between the blocs of power and it was possible to get to the West. That was not exactly right, but in the following months it was the catalyst for a wave of refugees and was to have a drastic impact. Events took a turn at the start of July when the Communist Party in China advanced violently on people who were protesting about the conditions there. These actions were even publicly praised by SED leader Egon Krenz. By the end of the month, thousands had left the "Workers' and Peasants' State" and turned their backs on it for good. When summer arrived, the floodgates really opened and the numbers increased dramatically. Things came to a head: years of pent-up discontent, the SED's obstinacy and rumours of the possibility to go to the West. The internal pressure that had been building up for such a long time found an outlet.

Since the border to West Germany was not nearly as open as some assumed it to be, another way out was found: the West German embassies in the Eastern bloc. In Budapest, Prague and Warsaw, the embassies were all completely flooded with

frustrated–but at the same time determined–GDR citizens. People climbed over the fences and simply refused to leave again. In order to limit the diplomatic implications, a number of embassies were simply officially closed. That, however, did not stop people from continuing to climb over the fences. The situation became truly dramatic. By midsummer, in temperatures of more then 30 degrees, thousands of men, women and children camped out in the open, in tents or other forms

^ *A first hole in the Iron Curtain. Around 600 GDR citizens escape from Hungary to Austria on 19 August 1989.*

of makeshift shelter. In Prague alone, there were more than 10,000 East Germans cramped within the embassy walls.

Images of the events went around the world. All summer, the images delegitimised the SED and the system it had created. After all, how desperate did people have to be in order to put themselves in such a situation? This inevitably led to a second question: how awful must the conditions in the GDR really be? Since the leaders were not able to come up with any means of stopping the adverse mass movement, they put on the emergency brakes at the end of September and allowed the ref-

^ *The West German embassy in Prague. Refugees have left everything behind and face an uncertain future.*

ugees to flee to West Germany. When the West German Foreign Minister Hans-Dietrich Genscher announced this from the balcony at the embassy in Prague, his words were drowned out by loud cheers. The embassies in Prague and Warsaw were vacated on the same evening and the people were taken to West Germany via train.

The SED believed that the situation was now under control. This could not have been further from the truth. Just a few days later, thousands more people had once again gathered at the embassies. More and more people wanted to get out of the "Workers' and Peasants' State" and their leaders reacted with more and more stubbornness. They made a cynical announcement in relation to the refugees: "Through their actions, they have all stamped on our moral values and ostracised themselves from our society. No tears shall be shed on their behalves."[41] With this comment, Honecker and his leading party members made it clear that they were not prepared to contemplate their own mistakes. It also meant that absolutely nothing in the GDR was going to change any time soon. The people were not prepared to silently accept this any longer. Dynamics of change were growing rapidly in response to government's rigidity.

Events that had been intensely followed by the entire world had, until now, been outside of Germany. With its next deci-

41 Neues Deutschland, 2 October 1989, p. 2.

^ *Genscher: "We have come here today to tell you that you are free to leave..." There are huge cheers.*

sions, the SED was to change that and the revolutionary spark was going to leap over to home territory. At the start of October, the SED allowed more refugees at the Prague embassy to leave for West Germany, but insisted that they had to leave over GDR territory. As a result and instead of taking a direct route, the trains, filled with people, took a route which led them through what would later become Saxony and Thuringia. At the same time, the party closed the border to Czechoslovakia. The GDR citizens were in a sealed off country – and the trains leaving Prague suddenly seemed like the only way out. Eery scenes were played out along the route as people continually tried to

get inside the trains. Civil war-like scenes were seen around Central Station in Dresden; cars were burning. Nothing like it had ever happened before. It was clear how determined the people were to change, what was to them, an unacceptable situation. It also showed that those in power did not think about changes. The conflict of interest was intensifying.

By now, there had even been some developments within the GDR; in particular, the civic opposition had begun to organise itself. After the elections in May, the Stasi had estimated that there were about 160 opposition groups throughout the country, and these groups were now beginning to form an effective network. It was of great advantage that most of the people leading the way had known each other for years and there was a great deal of trust between them. There was a host of parties been founded throughout the GDR. The people's movement "Democracy Now" (DJ), the "Democratic Awakening" (DA) and the "Social Democratic Party in the GDR" (SDP)–they were all founded in early autumn 1989 and attacked the SED's autocracy. Alongside these organisations, which gradually began to form nationwide, the "New Forum" (NF) gained an outstanding position. Like no other institution, it became the voice of the frustrated people. The New Forum expressed it did not wish to be a party, but a wide political coalition movement. By the end of the year, 200,000 people had signed its founding demand entitled "The Time is Now–New Start 89". The paper talked of transforming the GDR, not, however, abolishing it.

Already on 4 October–at a time when not all of the participating groups had officially been formed–a socalled contact

group of the opposition met for the first time in Berlin. Its job was to take over coordination so that individual participants would not be immediately crushed by the SED. During its first meeting, the contact group announced a joint declaration in which, among other things, implementation of human rights and democratic votes were demanded. In doing so, it challenged the GDR's social system, as both demands were not at all consistent with the SED dictatorship. At the end of September, those in power finally acknowledged the very real situation which had since developed: "On assessing the situation, we will have to consequently assume that the actions of our enemies at home and abroad have reached a new level."[42]

By early October, things had further developed in the GDR. Alongside the wave of refugees, a plethora of new parties were founded, but oppositional initiatives remained illegal until this point. Despite widespread approval, this was still a minority. It was also by no means the case that these initiatives challenged the SED or even socialism in the GDR. The aim was most often to bring about changes to the current situation through reform and not a revolution to overthrow the system. However, the tide turned within a few days.

42 Protocol from 26 September 1989 during a conference with minister Mittig, in: BStU, BV Potsdam, AKG 617, Bl. 164.

^ *From early autumn 1989, there is a wave of opposition coalitions. The New Forum seen here at the start of September.*

The fact that until now the SED leadership and the Stasi had generally acted reservedly (except in Dresden) was above all down to one thing: the GDR was to celebrate its 40th birthday on 7 October. High-ranking guests from numerous countries were expected and nothing should dampen the mood. Gorbachev, who also made his way to East Germany, had warned that life punishes those who come too late. This appeared to be nothing more than one of the usual platitudes of daily politics, but it would quickly become something more. While party and state leaders celebrated themselves in East Berlin's Palace of the Republic and Honecker emphasised that socialism on German soil was steadfast, trouble was brewing on the streets outside.

Since the elections in May, a few tireless people had been gathering at Alexanderplatz on the seventh day of each month to remember the fraud that had taken place. When state security forces went to move in with their usual ruthlessness, protests broke out. A public festival was also being held at the same time, many of its visitors also joined in and revolted. The courage shown by a few impinged upon the, until now, silent and dissatisfied masses and a fateful dynamic was created. Right away, a protest march was formed and it made its way to the nearby Palace of the Republic. It continued to grow and energetically demanded democracy for the GDR. Once the security forces had managed to push the protestors

^ *Berlin 7 October 1989. The protests have reached the capital city. The people make their discontent known.*

out of the city centre, they were brutally attacked. Men, women and youngsters were surrounded, set upon with batons and water cannons, and arrested. Literally anyone could be targeted, all laws were meaningless and rules were arbitrary. Similar scenes were repeated the following evening. Under these changed circumstances, the SED leadership was heading for disaster.

Similar scenes were also seen on this evening in scores of other towns across the GDR, from Rostock in Mecklenburg, to Plauen in Saxony. There were even protests against the party in small villages. In Großröhrsdorf, Saxony, for example, almost 50 young people came together after a dance and they energetically demanded change and chanted: "We want out". Even here, action was taken against them: 43 demonstrators were arrested.

By 7 October, something had been put in motion that would not be stopped: the people took over the streets calling for an end to the dictatorship. German flags were seen for the first time. The question on everyone's lips, however, was what was going to happen in Leipzig two days later. Monday demonstrations had been taking place here for the past few months and they were getting more and more resentful towards the current situation. On 9 October, the time had come. There had been rumours all day about approaching tanks and reserve supplies of blood. After the events in Berlin, it was well

^ *Party and state leaders refuse to talk. They celebrate their regime and brutally deploy security services.*

within the realms of possibility that events in Leipzig could lead to a bloody escalation. Indeed, around 8,000 security forces had been redeployed to the city, orders to actually deploy them, however, had still not been given. After the events of the last few days, the citizens in the GDR no longer had any reservations and they flocked to Leipzig. More than 70,000 people filled the streets and were chanting what had become familiar slogans: "No violence", "We are the people". The seemingly almighty security services had to surrender to the sheer number of people, and the evening remained peaceful. No conclusive decisions had been made, but the message sent out from Leipzig was clear: the people, who had been silent and resigned for so long, would no longer be kept quiet, the SED leadership became the people's prey and hurtled towards its downfall. For decades, the party had projected an image that it was the highest power, and now the people made it clear what they thought of this: nothing.

This finally dawned on the innermost circle of those in power. An ineffectual palace coup followed on 17 October which did see Honecker deposed, but, this aside, there was little change. Just a few weeks earlier, such a move could have had cathartic consequences. Now it had happened but for the people on the streets it was too late and meant nothing. Furthermore Egon Krenz, of all people, had been selected as suc-

^ *Plauen in the Vogtlandkreis, 7 October 1989. Water cannons are deployed. The demonstrators reply: "We will return!"*

cessor. As Honecker's deputy for years and chairman of the central election commission, he was responsible for the deception in May and he had praised his Chinese comrades for their bloody action in June. He stood wholeheartedly for the old system, and yet he was supposed to be the symbol of a new start. This absurd transition of power was fuel enough to make the people take to the streets once more and their numbers increased dramatically.

On 4 November, the largest demonstration ever in the GDR's history took place. In the centre of East Berlin, especially at Alexanderplatz, many hundreds of thousands of people gathered and publicly demonstrated their opinions. SED speakers were booed and suggestions from the oppositional people's movement were cheered. Amid a sea of banners, the protesters demanded fundamental changes in politics. The events were broadcast live on GDR television (which would have been unimaginable a few weeks earlier) and led to the involvement of many more people. Eventually, one event was to shake up world history entirely.

^ *120,000 people turn up to the Monday Demonstrations in Leipzig on 16 October 1989. The people conquer the streets.*

^ *The demonstrations in the GDR intensify phenomenally throughout the GDR at the end of October. Leipzig and Berlin remain the centres.*

Information vom Verband der Theaterschaffenden

Demonstration

gegen Gewalt und fuer verfassungsmaessige Rechte

(Demonstration ist offiziell angemeldet)

Zeit: 4.11.89 10 Uhr
Treffpunkt: ADN-Gebaeude

(Mollstrasse/Prenzlauer Allee)

Plakate sind erwuenscht

^ *The demonstrations are still all illegal, but that changes in Berlin on 4 November 1989. The response is enormous.*

SDP
VOLK

^ *Officially registered by artists, and granted by the SED due to increasing pressure, thousands upon thousands gather at a protest.*

GELD
FÜR
LEISTU

^ *The entire inner-city is a sea of people, expectations are great. The mood is tense but cheerful at the same time.*

Tschüß

SED

^ *East Berlin, 4 November 1989. Demonstration scenes.*

THE FALL OF THE WALL

On 9 November 1989, obviously astonished, writer Walter Kempowski wrote in his diary: "The Wall might actually fall."[43] What had until now seemed impossible was becoming reality. The fact that it suddenly happened, as well as how it happened, was, again, thanks to the poor crisis management on the SED's part.

9 November was a cool autumn Thursday. The border to Czechoslovakia had been opened again a few days ago and people were leaving the GDR in flocks. Indeed, the SED had by now recognised the need for change, but could this be believed? For far too long the party had made promises which were never kept. Furthermore, it was true that a lot had happened over the last few months, but, theoretically, the SED still held power. The old structures were starting to shake, but it would not be impossible for them to be stabilised again. And so, many people continued to leave their country.

The government had to find a solution before everyone left. New travel regulations were promised which would finally allow GDR citizens to visit any country of their choice. When the respective draft was published on 5 November, it provoked nothing but outrage. In theory, it should have been possible to travel immediately. However, this had to be granted first by the SED administration. This authoritarian process was at one with the old party line and the people no longer wanted to be controlled by a non-transparent government or restricted

43 Walter Kempowski, Alkor. Tagebuch 1989, Munich 2003, p. 500.

in their travel. Furthermore, the draft put limits on travel time and did not mention where the necessary funds were to come from. It was clear that nobody would get far with the East German Mark. After the longstanding government had resigned under increasing pressure on 7 November, the SED leaders tried to gain control again with the aid of a large-scale event stressing the feeling of togetherness among the GDR citizens. On 8 November, the party's Central Committee met. In order to demonstrate transparency, as well as making it possible to announce decisions quickly, press conferences were arranged for the evenings after each meeting. At 6:00pm, the press conferences were broadcast live on GDR TV and radio. On the first day, the SED's most powerful group, its Politburo, resigned and that attracted a lot of attention. The following day was spent picking apart the new travel regulations both publicly and behind the scenes. The paper was ready by the afternoon and it was read out to all attending comrades by Krenz.

It ultimately came down to newly named government spokesman Günter Schabowski to make an announcement to the world press gathered in East Germany.

The new suggestions were geared above all towards easing the pressure bearing down on the GDR. From 10 November, all GDR citizens would be allowed to travel without having to present special reasons. Such trips, however, would still have

^ *9 November 1989, evening. Günter Schabowski on his way to the press conference. Nobody knows yet what is about to happen.*

to be applied for. Police stations responsible for dealing with applications were given details before they were made public so that they could prepare themselves for the wave of people expected to turn up the next morning.

Schabowski had almost brought the one hour press conference to an end when an Italian journalist asked about the new travel regulations. Schabowski seemed overwhelmed as he spoke, he stuttered as he read from his prepared text and tripped on his own words. The impression he gave was everything but that of supremacy. The journalist, on the other hand, knew that something sensational was happening. After more than 28 years, the GDR was allowing what was almost freedom of movement over what had been a deadly border. At this time, shortly before 7:00pm, nobody could have imagined what was to happen the following evening.

Schabowski's answer to two questions set the ball rolling for events in the coming hours which would lead to the Fall of the Berlin Wall. First of all, not only did he confirm the suspension of all travel regulations pertaining to the inner-German border, but also to divided Berlin. Secondly, and his reasons for doing so are still widely debated today, he disregarded the deadline for the changes to take effect. Asked from when the regulations would be valid, he replied with words that would go down in history: "immediately, without delay". The press conference was being broadcast live, the journalists were alive with excitement, but, for now, on the streets of

^ *Schabowski babbles his instrumental words: "That comes into effect, according to my information, immediately, without delay."*

Berlin, nothing happened. However, once the West German evening news had reported that the border was (more or less) open, the first curious people began to set off to take a look. The numbers would grow and grow in the coming hours. There were particularly large crowds gathered at the crossing point on Bornholmer Straße between the heavily populated city districts of Prenzlauer Berg (East) and Wedding (West). The crowds referred to Schabowski and the news in the media and demanded free access to the West which, initially, was denied. There was a great sense of uncertainty among the guards. They had neither received any kind of information about the procedure, nor had they been given clear orders from above. Attempts to ease the situation by letting individual people over the border–who were silently expatriated during the process–actually had the opposite effect. Those left behind just pushed even harder. At around 11:30pm, there was no other choice: the border guards decided for themselves to open the gates and let people through. The same process was completed on all other inner-city crossing points by midnight. What had seemed completely impossible just a few weeks ago suddenly became reality: there were holes in the Wall and people everywhere could pass freely. Nobody could say what would happen next. However, one thing was for certain: the general setup had changed dramatically overnight.

^ *The evening Bornholmer Straße became famous worldwide. The first part of the Wall was opened here on 9 November; there is no going back.*

^ *People flock to the West, the Wall has fallen. A new species is born: the "Wall-pecker".*

^ *At the Brandenburg Gate, which had been a symbol of division for 28 years, people climb on top of the Wall and celebrate.*

^ *No words.*

TEAR
THE
AND

^ *The Wall does prove to be the start of a chain reaction, even if not all walls fell.*

^ *In the following weeks, countless crossings are also made along the inner-German border. The euphoria for the unexpected*

changes is clear to see on both sides, like here at this crossing between Ellrich (Thuringia) and Walkenried (Lower Saxony)

DEM DEUTSCHEN VOLKE

3 OCTOBER 1990
GERMAN UNITY

According to internal records, more then half a million people crossed the border from East to West Berlin on 10 November 1989. By the next day, more than 600,000 visas enabling the journeys over the border were issued in the capital city of the "Workers' and Peasants' State" alone. However, nobody could say with certainty exactly how many people had made the trip across the border at this time. A happy sort of chaos and euphoria were the order of the day, and the exact overview had long since been lost. People wrapped their arms around each other in joyous hugs. Despite the enormous changes in the previous months, not many people had thought it possible that the Wall would be opened in the foreseeable future. It had, however, actually happened. Everything seemed possible.

^ *10 November 1989. The situation is still not clear. For this reason, many GDR citizens are trying to get visas to go to West Germany.*

It began to dawn on more and more people that fundamental changes were just around the corner. On the same day the Wall fell, the opposition's contact group came up with a practical suggestion for the public: a round table should be formed. Representatives from the SED and the new groups could sit at the table to discuss and find solutions to the biggest problems. It was clear that the hitherto existing structure was no longer suitable and this was an opportunity to create a period of stability.

The SED leadership was quick to turn down the round table suggestions. It was claimed by the SED leadership that the contact group had two aims with its plans to form a round table, neither of which was acceptable from their point of view: a constitutional reform and free elections. After more than four decades of autocracy, giving up power was completely and utterly inconceivable to Krenz and his top officials. The country was in upheaval and they were the

^ *At the same time, people at the Brandenburg Gate are making history. The world's press is abuzz and reporting live.*

only ones not moving forward, they still believed they had everything under control. However, in the next few weeks, it became all too clear that they did not. An example of this was the appearance of one individual who had embodied the GDR for years: Erich Mielke. As minister for the Stasi, he was responsible for surveillance, oppression and taking away rights in the "Workers' and Peasants' State". People's careers were ruined on his demand, he never shied away from fighting opponents of the SED dictatorship (or people who he considered to be opponents) with every method available to him. He appeared before the People's Chamber (Parliament of the GDR) on 13 November 1989 and tried to calm the situation and shift the focus of attention to the future. His appearance was a disaster. What remained was the image of a stammering old man who was no longer in touch with reality and who legitimised his actions by claiming they were out of his love for all people: "I love, I love everyone. (Laughter) I do, I assure you...believe me! Believe me!"[44]

His appearance had devastating consequences for his ministry. By no later then the start of November, increasing numbers had taken to the streets to demand an end to the Stasi. Those

44 Acc. to: Deutschland Archiv. Zeitschrift für Fragen der DDR und der Deutschlandpolitik, no. 1/1990, p. 121.

^ *An appearance with consequences. Mielke in front of the People's Parliament after decades of serving as minister for the Stasi. This appearance had a devastating impact.*

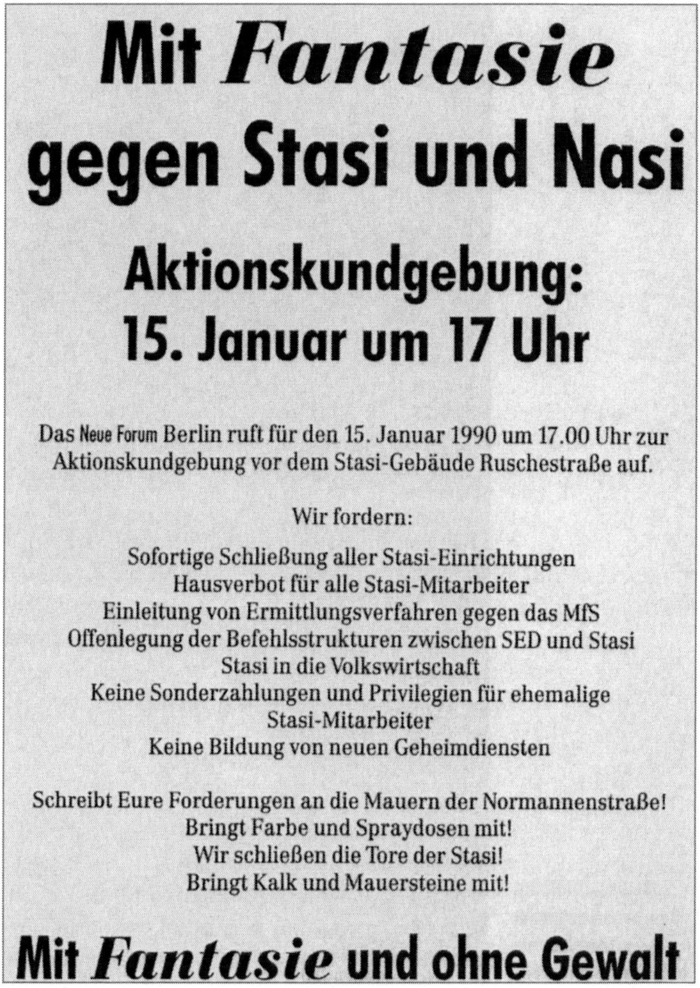

Mit *Fantasie* gegen Stasi und Nasi

Aktionskundgebung:
15. Januar um 17 Uhr

Das Neue Forum Berlin ruft für den 15. Januar 1990 um 17.00 Uhr zur Aktionskundgebung vor dem Stasi-Gebäude Ruschestraße auf.

Wir fordern:

Sofortige Schließung aller Stasi-Einrichtungen
Hausverbot für alle Stasi-Mitarbeiter
Einleitung von Ermittlungsverfahren gegen das MfS
Offenlegung der Befehlsstrukturen zwischen SED und Stasi
Stasi in die Volkswirtschaft
Keine Sonderzahlungen und Privilegien für ehemalige Stasi-Mitarbeiter
Keine Bildung von neuen Geheimdiensten

Schreibt Eure Forderungen an die Mauern der Normannenstraße!
Bringt Farbe und Spraydosen mit!
Wir schließen die Tore der Stasi!
Bringt Kalk und Mauersteine mit!

Mit *Fantasie* und ohne Gewalt

at the top were obviously shaken. Neither Mielke's complete withdrawal from politics, nor the sudden attempt at honesty changed anything. The demand was getting louder: "Make the Stasi do real work". For the time being, nobody dared to directly confront the almighty Stasi, but that was about to change. At the start of November, Mielke had ordered that extensive records from his database be destroyed. Smoke had been bellowing non-stop from the chimneys since then, the shredders were in action and the evidence was being destroyed. That was

^ *An appeal with consequences. The New Forum calls to the people: the Stasi's villainous work should no longer be tolerated.*

the final straw: on 4 December 1989, outraged citizens across the country stormed Stasi property in order to prevent further destruction of the files. Until then, this had been completely unimaginable, it took place without blood shed and showed just how much circumstances had already changed. The SED made many attempts to save its long serving instrument of power, but they all failed. The events surrounding the Stasi were also of advantage to the SED. They helped to divert attention away from those who were actually responsible for the widespread oppression: the SED itself.

The confrontations with the Stasi were bitter and dragged out. A significant moment came on 15 January 1990. It was on this day that demonstrators occupied the Stasi headquarters in Lichtenberg (a district in Berlin). Occupying this building was like cutting an artery: the Stasi could no longer function. Whether or not anyone else was involved in the events that followed–be it the Stasi itself, Western secret services or other shady characters–that is still a hot topic of discussion today. It took a few more months, until June 1990, until the Stasi was history. Many mistakes were made during the process of dismantling the Stasi, the destruction of electronic storage devices for example. However, the process on the whole must be considered a success. An instrument made up of almost 90,000 full-time workers, which a year before had been considered un-

^ *The beginning of the end. Civil rights activists occupy a Stasi regional office in Erfurt on 4 December.*

touchable, had been brought down without blood loss. Nothing like this had ever been seen before.

In December 1989, the SED was fighting for its own survival. Formally the SED still held all important posts it had held before, but the people had threateningly turned away and made increasingly radical demands. The call for reform had turned into a revolutionary mass movement. The demonstrators did not break, hundreds of thousands of people were taking part by now and they were not going to be bullied any more. The demand for the unification of the two German states was getting louder.

The more the opposing unions fought it out in public, the more the reputation of the SED suffered. Discussions were now being held about exactly what the party, with its monopoly over information and freedom of speech, had been hiding: illegal actions committed by those with political power, corruption, tyranny. This caused rebellion among party members; they denied their decades of allegiance. Furthermore, the longstanding accomplices in the SED, the bloc parties and mass organisations were increasingly distancing themselves from each other. They were also beginning to worry about their very existence. GDR citizens continued to leave the state in their thousands. While ever there were no radical and irreversible reforms, nothing was going to change and help stop the con-

^ *The Stasi headquarters are stormed on 15 January 1990. The difficult task of breaking up the Stasi is making great progress.*

stant flow of people leaving. Nobody believed the empty promises any more. The country was hemorrhaging people and the structures were collapsing.

Under these conditions, the SED leadership changed its strategy. The old guard of the party was relieved of its duties by early December, and a few days later Krenz also had to step down. He had taken the post with such high hopes, but just a few weeks later these hopes had been dashed. Hopes were now pinned on someone new: Hans Modrow. Under his leadership, the party, which technically still ruled the state, wanted to create a modern, cosmopolitan outward appearance. In line with this, the SED's claim to leadership was deleted from the East German Constitution. Those in power also agreed to cooperate at the central Round Table. The first meeting was held on 7 December 1989 in East Berlin. Equal representatives were present from old and new parties, as well as other institutions. The talks became the focal point of the political debates. The endless meetings were broadcast on live television and the people were engrossed. As was to be expected, the meetings were extremely controversial. The SED clung on to its power, opposing civil societies fought against the SED and made a point of highlighting the fact that the party was responsible for the GDR's ailing state. By mid-March 1990, during a total of 16 meetings, the Round Table settled a vast number of matters, moderated conflicts and submitted new draft legislations,

^ *The first Round Table meetings are held on 7 December 1989. The old powers try to proceed tactically in order outmanoeuvre the changes.*

among which was a draft for an electoral law (not, as is often claimed, a draft constitution for a reformed GDR). The People's Parliament passed the electoral legislation which became the basis for the elections for the next People's Parliament. The date was set for 18 March 1990. They were to be the first free elections in GDR territory.

^ *With the meetings being broadcast live, the opposition has created a forum where it was clear to see to what extent the SED was to blame for the situation.*

"WE ARE ONE PEOPLE!"

Our country is in the midst of a deep crisis. We cannot and do not want to live like we have been living up to now." These were the opening sentences of an appeal made to the East German people during a press conference on 28 November 1989. It was signed by 31 representatives, most of them prominent figures in the worlds of art, culture and politics. The appeal was entitled "For Our Country" and asked how things were to continue in the rebelling GDR. It was claimed that either the autonomy of the state could be kept and "a solidly united community" formed "in which freedom and social justice, freedom for the individual, freedom of movement for everyone and environmental preservation were all held up." Or "the beginning of a sellout of our material and moral values, as well as the German Democratic Republic sooner or later being taken over by the Federal Republic of Germany" had to be "tolerated". It was claimed that this would be initiated by "influential circles from West German politics and economy". The signatories–with a large share of opposisionists among them–were pushing for the first option: the continued existence of the GDR.

The appeal highlights the dilemma the revolutionary developments were now facing. The situation was a result of the masses of people leaving the GDR, it had been politicised by the opposing groups and was in search of a goal. The road ahead was fiercely disputed and since the Wall had fallen it looked like it could go in one of two directions: keeping the GDR, or unifying the two German states. In retrospect, it had

to seem extremely naïve to think that it was possible to achieve a united community, full of peace and justice in the "Workers' and Peasants' State." This was, however, the declaration of a quest which was hard pressed for time and suffering from a lack of background information. Which "material and moral values" were to be used to build the basis for autonomous progression? After more than 40 years of SED dictatorship, the country was materially and morally bankrupt.

Nevertheless, times of revolution are also times for utopian ideas, and many people thought the time had come to realise their dreams. They were mostly people who had grown up in the GDR and who harboured hatred and complete rejection towards the mechanisms of a market economy. A new debate quickly flared up about a "third way" between socialism and capitalism. However, nobody was really able to divulge details about how this should look and work.

This was already the debate for a minority. After the Fall of the Wall, the majority began to move quickly in a different direction. What had previously been looming among a handful of people was a matter of public interest by the end of November 1989: the demand for both German states to be unified could be heard at increasing numbers of demonstrations. It had been proven months before in Großwudicke ("let's pull down the Wall now") that these kinds of thoughts were widespread. Now the dams were gradually breaking. From the outset, there were worries about the challenges the future had in store. The decades of SED propaganda against the Federal Republic had

^ *There are also opponents to a speedy unification. However, they are a small minority.*

left their mark. Furthermore, there were very real threats: it was now becoming clearer how unfit the economy was to compete alongside others. This meant there was a threat of high unemployment. The Federal Republic could not be held responsible for that, it was the fault of those who had ruled the GDR. The Federal Republic's political elite were beginning to recognise the possibilities that were suddenly opening up. Indeed, the possibility and demand for reunification had always been valid in the West, but by the time of Honecker's visit to Bonn, hardly anyone believed that it would become reality in the foreseeable future. Suitable plans for the event did not exist and a period of improvisation began.

The most decisive act came from Federal Chancellor Kohl on 28 November–the same day as the announcement of the "For Our Country" appeal–he presented a ten-point plan which would result in unification. At the time, however, the chancellor assumed that ten years would have to pass first; in-

^ *Leipzig, 11 December 1989. The mood has changed dramatically. Reunification of the two German states is the main priority.*

deed, most people would have considered even this to be optimistic. But other events were about to take place thick and fast. At the start of December, Mikhail Gorbachev and American President George H. W. Bush declared the Cold War between the power blocs over. This relieved tensions in international politics and opened up the door for new courses of action. The Ministry for State Security's offices were taken over, the central Round Table meetings were held, and more and more wrong doings from 40 years of the "dictatorship of the proletariat" came to light. At the same time, during a special party conference in December, the SED changed its name to PDS (Party of Democratic Socialism) and replaced those at the top: it appeared the SED was stabilising itself once more. However, the overall economic situation got steadily worse and people continued to leave the country in huge numbers. There was a lack of clear perspectives.

The way things were to go became apparent in Dresden on 19 December. Even after this day, it was still not laid down in stone exactly which path should be taken. However, the images that came from Saxony's metropolitan city of Dresden were of great symbolic power and helped to speed up the process. Federal Chancellor Kohl arrived to meet with premier Modrow. The people of Dresden gave him a warm welcome. Black-red-gold flags (without the GDR emblem) lined the streets. Con-

^ *Dresden, 19 December 1989. Chancellor Kohl is a cunning politician, he recognises the signs of the times and acts respectively.*

stant cries of "Germany, Germany" and "We are one people/ nation" could be heard. As a power-seeking politician, Kohl, who had to stand for election in 1990, quickly realised what he stood to gain from a fast reunion of both German states. At the same time, he appeared to be actually emotionally and deeply moved. There were to be many, in part extremely complicated, problems to be solved, but the aim of his political life had now finally been unequivocally defined: reunification.

To what extent he represented the wish of the majority of people in the GDR would be shown during the election on 18 March 1990. In the run up to the elections, numerous parties and coalitions were formed, and German unity was on the agenda for almost every party. After consultation with Moscow, even the PDS recognised this. It assumed, however, that the process would be long-term and made up of many stages. A number of policy decisions were also made before the elections which also favoured unity. In mid-February, both German states agreed upon the instillation of a unified commission of experts that would prepare for a German-German currency union and economic unity. In the same month, the Second World War Allies announced that they were prepared to discuss issues around foreign policy in relation to the process of unity. This was known as the "Two-Plus-Four" negotiations (the four victorious powers plus the two German states). It was clear that reunification would not take place without their approval.

At this point in time, however, all negotiations were made under one condition: The GDR was not commanded by a democratically authorised government. A "government of national responsibility" was called for at the start of February, eight ministers without portfolio were part of it, and had come from the people's movement. This was sensational and, until a few months before, had been unimaginable. However, even this cabinet lacked the democratic legitimacy of free voting. And so, for the time being, everything was running up to 18 May.

The increasingly intense election campaign sped up changes which had been on the cards for a while. The balance of power shifted: away from the few hierarchical, decentralised organisations and often impromptu citizens' movements, towards parties based on a democratic parliamentary system. This was of great advantage to all those organisations which

received support from the Federal Republic or those which could revert back to established structures (such as the former block parties).

The result of the election was a clear reflection of this. Contrary to all election forecasts, it was not the Social Democratic

^ *Election campaign for 18 March 1990. The warning voices fall on deaf ears, supporters of a rapid unification are triumphant.*

Party that came out as the victor with almost 22 percent, but the conservative “Alliance for Germany”. Alongside the old CDU block party, it belonged to the newly founded Democratic Awakening and the German Social Union. Alongside the newly founded Democratic Awakening and the German Social Union, the old CDU bloc party was also part of the Alliance for

Germany. The electoral alliance fostered the slogan "Freedom and prosperity–never again socialism". It had enjoyed huge support from the Federal German CDU and called for a swift unification of the two German states. The fact that the alliance was able to secure almost 50 percent of the votes made it clear that this was the direction in which things were heading. Alli-

^ *Erfurt, March 1990. Willy Brandt, SPD icon on campaign trail. This is where he had met the GDR's prime minister in 1970.*

ance 90, in contrast, which united three of the most significant instigators of the Peaceful Revolution (one of them being the New Forum), gained less than three percent of the votes. Even what had become the PDS out of the SED was far more successful: it gained 16 percent of the votes. The result of the election pointed the way forward and also answered another question. Until then, intense discussions had been going on which focused on *how* the states could be unified. Legally, there were two possibilities: the ascension of the GDR to Federal German territory of German Basic Law, or to draft a new joint constitution. The "Alliance for Germany" had campaigned avidly for the first possibility and it was clear that the majority of voters also wanted this. The decision had been made. It was no longer a question of if and how, but simply a matter of *how quickly* the unification of the two states would take place.

^ *The former bloc party CDU looks for its own path for the future. It goes on to win the East German general election.*

THE PATH TO GERMAN UNITY

A grand coalition was formed in mid-April 1990 after difficult negotiations. As well as the "Alliance for Germany", the social democrats and the liberals were also members. The government was made up of a broad political base, which seemed like a good idea given the task ahead. Next to everyday politics, the cabinet had one single task to complete: a speedy reunification. But that was even more complicated than it already sounded. After all, the entire country had undergone its own developmental process for 40 years. Its structures, political culture and social identity differed fundamentally from those in the Federal Republic of Germany. This country had to make preparations for a political merger. Fierce debates about exactly how this should be done were long and drawn out. In effect, the decision had been made at the election and that predetermined the way forward. If the GDR wished to join the West German sphere of influence, it had to approximate West Germany as far as possible in all areas–and it had to do so as fast as possible. Thousands of people continued to leave for the West, stability could only be achieved if fundamental changes were made soon.

The first crucial step in this direction was a treaty which brought about an economic, monetary and social union. When it came into effect on 1 July 1990, to a great extent, the GDR adopted the economic and legal order of the Federal Republic. For the people, the biggest change was the Deutschmark becoming legal tender. Many people had been demanding this for months and now it was reality. Long queues formed out-

side banks as people went about converting their accounts from one currency to the other. Depending on age, private bankers were able to exchange up to 6,000 East German marks at an exchange rate of 1:1. Larger sums of money were subject to an exchange rate of 1:2. Salaries, pensions, rent and other regular payments were also subject to an exchange rate of 1:1. Overnight the shops were filled with Western produce; it was to be a tough few years for local produce. The people were fulfilling wishes they had thought about for years. It was the start of a free-enterprise system which could often be fierce. Car dealerships became common sites on East German streets, fast food outlets sprung up everywhere. People were trying to make a quick fortune with dubious businesses.

This consumerist orientated behaviour is easy to explain when one takes the previous decades of shortages into account. However, not everyone from the GDR shared this sentiment. Some, who glorified the values of socialism, warned that the GDR was selling itself out and looked down on the allegedly uninhibited people: those people who brought about the Peaceful Revolution in the first place. As is common during such periods of transition, there was a mixture of joy and denial, activism and apathy. While some threw themselves enthusiastically into the new way of life, others warned against it. Already by March 1990, a concerned federal citizen from North Rhine-Westphalia had written to the New Forum to give the East Germans some serious advice. Attempts should be made for

^ *Ahead of the currency union, the shelves in GDR shops are stripped and filled with goods from West Germany.*

> "at least a part of the GDR to try and evade the next disaster, so it can remain independent and evolve independently ...Since not all citizens of the GDR want to be part of the GDR's integration into the Federal Republic (FRG), the Eastern part of the GDR should become its own state, big enough in size for all those who wish to remain in the GDR."[45]

Nothing became of this and measures to unify the states continued swiftly. On 1 July 1990, when controls at the border were stopped, one more step towards reunification had been achieved. The People's Parliament had already passed the "Treuhandgesetz" (Trusteeship Act) which determined the conversion of the East German economy according to the rules of a market economy–above all, this meant privatisation.

A second act was to follow the first: the "Einigungsvertrag" (Unification Treaty). Signed on 31 August 1990, it rendered East German legislation permanently inoperative and also stipulated changes in the "Grundgesetz" (German con-

45 Letter from 15 March 1990, in: Tina Krone (Ed.), »Sie haben so lange das Sagen, wie wir es dulden«. Briefe an das Neue Forum, September 1989–March 1990, Berlin 1999, p. 379f.

^ *The Deutschmark arrives. One of the people's central demands is realised on 1 July 1990. There is, however, some apprehension.*

stitution). The act planned for the formation of federal states in GDR territory (instead of the districts which had existed since 1952), set out measures for public administration, regulated issues around property and debt, and much more. Berlin was defined as a federal state and capital city. A decision as to where the parliament and government should sit was, however, to be made later. The act also named the 3 October 1990 as unification day. From now on, 3 October would be recognised as the Day of German Unity and celebrated as a national public holiday. There were two central arguments surrounding the Unification Treaty and they led to emotional debates and significant delays. The differences between the East and the West

^ *Travel agents pop up everywhere after the currency union. Interest in foreign countries from the GDR is great.*

were manifested in the arguments. These differences were easy to oversee or underestimate amid the all-encompassing euphoria. There was the question of legal time limits for abortion and also a question about what should now be done with files made and collected by the Stasi. It was, however, possible to find workable solutions even for these problems. With the approval of both parties–despite "no" votes on both sides–the Unification Treaty became valid. Further hurdles were overcome as a result.

German unity was only possible because the victorious powers of the Second World War had signalled their willingness to agree to the course of events during the difficult "Two-Plus-Four Talks". France and Great Britain, in particular, had their reservations for historical reasons, and the Soviet Union feared a loss of influence in Central Europe. While it was relatively easy to dispel the fears of the Western Europeans, negotiations with the Soviet Union proved more difficult. The military alliance of the unified states became a focal point of the debates. Gorbachev was under political pressure in his own country. After compromises and concessions, he ultimately agreed that Germany should be allowed to decide upon its own alliances. It was clear to everyone what this meant in practice: the unified country would become a member of the Western defence community NATO, and the Soviet troops would retreat from German soil. The fact that both German states had recognised

^ *East Berlin, 31 August 1990. Wolfgang Schäuble, Lothar de Maizière and Günther Krause. The Unification Treaty is signed.*

the Oder–Neiße line to Poland helped to facilitate the compromise. With the signing of The Treaty on the Final Settlement with respect to Germany in Moscow on 12 September 1990, which established the authority of the unified state, the path to unification was clear.

And then it came, the Day of German Unity. Celebrations in honour of the GDR had taken place just one year earlier. Since then, world history had catapulted forward and the country was carried to its grave. There were mixed feelings about this. There were those who refused the moves for political reasons. There were those who were afraid of what the future held. There were those who had little faith in the promise of flourishing pastures for East Germany. There were those who had spent their entire lives in the GDR and did not like to imagine anything else. There were many more who did not want to be part of the general joy for many reasons–in both the East and the West.

There was, however, great joy. Despite the increasing deliberation, the majority of people appeared to be happy about unification and they expressed this. Black-red-gold dominated public spaces, there were private and official parties up and down the country. By 2 October, there was one ceremonial act after the other, the People's Parliament ceased its activities, both permanent representatives in Berlin and Bonn were closed, and the occupation of Berlin was ended. The "Fest der

^ *Negotiations between the two German states and the Allies in Bonn. Essential decisions are made here.*

Freiheit" (Celebration of Unity) was the main event and took place in front of the Reichstag. Thousands of people took part, including a small group of protesters against unification. At midnight on 3 October 1990, German unity was complete. The GDR, the self-proclaimed "Workers' and Peasants' State", was history.

^ *From promises of salvation, to the rubbish dump. The SED dictatorship ultimately fails.*

^ *Unity is complete on 3 October 1990. Reactions range from protests to church services.*

^ *The "Workers' and Peasants' state", a German possibility? The question is answered after almost 40 years.*

DANZIG

^ *2/3 October 1990. The main unification festivities in front of the Reichstag.*

EPILOGUE

TEH GDR AT THE END

The GDR was a child of the Second World War. When it was founded in October 1949, a lot had already been decided and the future trajectory had already been laid out. The Soviet Union guided the way and would do so almost until the end of the "Workers' and Peasants' State". When it gave up this role, the GDR also disappeared.

From the very start, repression and violence played an important role in the foundation and preservation of the SED dictatorship. People lost their lives, they were locked up in specially made prisons or camps. Every type of divergent behaviour was rigorously persecuted whenever the government felt it right. In this sense, the GDR was an illegitimate state which lacked basic human rights. The Party, the SED, not only decided everything to do with the country's well-being, it also decided the fate of each individual person where it saw necessary. Celebrities were no different to the "normal" workers and farmers, and individuals like Wolf Biermann could also be reprimanded. This suppressed both independent thinking and creativity and, in turn, the main requirements for dynamic, forward-looking developments were also suppressed. Marxist-Leninist ideology was and remained the only role model. Everyday life was continually adapted to fit in with these ideological requirements. Only after it had gone through this process of adaptation was any kind of reality taken seriously by those in power. This led to a distorted view of reality which ultimately prevented strategies being put in place which could have stabilised their own system.

Repression and violence, however, only make up one side of the coin. By destroying existing structures and established traditions, and persecuting both real and alleged opponents, the government created room for something new: destruction and reconstruction were bound tightly with each other. This established opportunities for both those who were forced to, and those who were prepared to go along with the necessary adjustments and, thereby, they played either an active or a passive part in the dictatorship. The SED leadership was, at times, capable of providing incentives and creating a mood of optimism. This provided its supporters with reasons to follow the party line, reasons based on opportunism, conviction or other, often very personal, matters. Any builder who obtained a piece of land after the Second World War could then be sure of his future survival–for this he had reason to be thankful. Every working-class child whose chances of a career had at first been limited would consider the SED appealing. Single parents profiting from state benefits including kindergarten places or time off work for housekeeping very rarely rebelled against what was taking place.

At the same time, such things made it easy to see the real motives behind the SED's actions: they were power strategies. Ideological redistribution aimed to create loyalty among the people and with it, stability for the state. Should this loyalty begin to waver, the government would act decisively. The consequences of this can be seen after the People's Uprising in 1953, after the Wall had been built in 1961 and also in the case of Biermann's expatriation. Loyalty could not be achieved with violence alone and for this reason there were continual phases of alleviated tension. During these phases, the SED would approach "its" people again, forego overly obvious propaganda, announce improvements in terms of materialism and create new visions for the future. The continuous switch from repression to cooperation can be seen throughout the GDR's history. And up until the mid-1970s, among a considerable section of society, this continuous switch was effective in creating a sense of (at least inactive) "sitting tight and holding on".

Then, however, there was a drop in momentum. It became clear very quickly that the adopted loyalty was (in the meantime) something very different: lethargy. Too often the party had made promises which were never fulfilled. Too often it had pointed out that a better future was just around the corner, without actually making the present state of things acceptable. At some point, many people had given up hope that their lives in the "Workers' and Peasants' State" would develop as they had wished; this was the view of an increasing number of people. Furthermore, there was the very perceptible phenomenon that life in the other German state was better. Even this undermined the SED's position in the long-term.

At the start of the GDR's final decade, the country was already worn out. Even worse: those in power had settled into the status quo. Creative minds continued to be suppressed and, during times of rampant shortages, every day life continued to get more difficult. "The people need cheap bread, a dry home, and work. As long as these three things are in place, nothing can happen to socialism."[46] This assessment by Honecker did have some basic character–and it was also basically wrong. In an increasingly modern world, this sort of pre-modern perception was not enough to create stability. It became clear at a rapidly growing rate that the regime had not managed to create a solid bond with its own people. The fact that almost every citizen belonged to a mass organisation, bloc party or other institution, and was therefore somehow integrated into the party, only simulated a solidarity which in reality did not exist. Even the loyalty among party officials was often fake and their public avowals to the "Workers' and Peasants' State" more of a strategy to move a career forward as opposed to an inner conviction. The socialist utopia was dead, but nobody had noticed it yet.

Hope reared its head one last time when signals of easing tensions were seen–from Moscow of all places. Mikhail Gorbachev's modest attempts at reform were followed closely and with great interest in the GDR. However, they were met with dismissal by Honecker and his leading comrades. It was clear by now that nothing, absolutely nothing about the increasingly frustrating circumstances in the "Workers' and Peasants' State" would change in the near future. This became a critical problem, as local officials were increasingly reporting to East Berlin: "We cannot find arguments to explain that to our col-

46 Acc. to: Steiner, Von Plan zu Plan, p. 216.

leagues. How is this to go on?"[47] Those in power remained stuck for an answer to this question until the very end. To a great extent, the GDR had become a meaningless, hollow and depressing construct by now, and little else was needed to catapult it into obscurity. The events that would do just this took place in early summer 1989. Gaining independent control of local elections activated oppositional powers, and the burgeoning wave of refugees (or more exactly: the images of it sent back to the GDR) led to ever increasing numbers of the population getting involved.

"We are accustomed to say, that the mass of men are unprepared; but improvement is slow, because the few are not materially wiser or better than the many."[48] This was written by American writer Henry David Thoreau in the middle of the 19th century. And now, the two were meeting. The "many" and the "few" were no longer under any kind of illusion and they began to act. The interaction quickly led to a dynamic the SED knew it could not oppose. Within a year, things that had once been unimaginable started to take shape. The Fall of the Wall and reunification are just the obvious parts; the democratisation of a dictatorship, the successful liquidation of an intelligence agency, and the high level of willingness among those who took part to embark upon such challenges, must also be mentioned here.

The GDR perished due to unkept promises. Its people did not want to be continually consoled with an undefined, unrealistic tomorrow. What began for many as a time of hope after the war, had ultimately lost its appeal. The longer the SED was able to maintain the illusion that it was in control of the situation, as well as to continue claiming it had half reasonable ideas for the future, the longer it could hope for supporters. Systematic mistakes made it harder and harder, and, in the end, prevented this completely. A party that suppresses personality but rewards naïve followers, a party that thinks it can lay down the rules for the smallest things and still thinks it is justified, is hardly able to react effectively to new challenges. A party that makes all of its decisions based on ideological

47 Letter from DBD party executive from 20 October 1986, in: BArch, DY 30/1867, Bl. 61.

48 Henry David Thoreau, Civil Disobedience and Other Essays, New York 1993, p. 5.

considerations eventually has to be marginalised. And if such a party should feel called upon to dictate an entire country, the options for the future are inevitably limited. Only when the people turn against the sovereign or when they spark off a (peaceful) revolution, only then will the power waver. Or it falls. Just as it did in the GDR.

^ *No words.*

APPENDIX

LIST OF ABBREVIATIONS

ABV	Community Policemen
BArch	German Federal Archives
BStU	Stasi Records Agency
BV	Stasi Regional Office
CDU	Christian Democratic Union
cf.	compare
DBD	Democratic Farmers' Party of Germany
DFD	Democratic Women's League of Germany
DWK	German Economic Commission
Ed.	Editor
FDGB	Free German Trade Union Federation
FDJ	Free German Youth
GDR	German Democratic Republic
GST	Sport and Technology Association
KPD	Communist Party of Germany
KPdSU	Communist Party of the Soviet Union
LDP	Liberal Democratic Party
LPG	Agricultural Production Cooperatives
MfS	Ministry for State Security, commonly known as the Stasi
NATO	North Atlantic Treaty Organization
NDPD	National Democratic Party of Germany (East Germany)
NÖS	New Economic System
NVA	National People's Army
n. d.	no date
p.	page
PDS	Party of Democratic Socialism
RHG	Robert-Havemann-Gesellschaft e. V.

SAPMO	Foundation Archives of Parties and Mass Organizations of the GDR in the Federal Archives
SBZ	Soviet Occupation Zone
SED	Socialist Unity Party of Germany
SKK	Soviet Control Commission
SMAD	Soviet Military Administration in Germany
SPD	Social Democratic Party of Germany
USSR	Soviet Union
UNESCO	United Nations Educational, Scientific and Cultural Organization
UN	United Nations
USA	United States of America
vol.	volume
WHO	World Health Organization

ADDITIONAL LITERATURE AND SOURCES

LIST OF ILLUSTRATIONS

ADDITIONAL LITERATURE AND SOURCES

Jens Gieseke, Die Stasi 1945–1990, Munich 2011.

Anna Kaminsky (Ed.), Orte des Erinnernp. Gedenkzeichen, Gedenkstätten und Museen zur Diktatur in SBZ und DDR, Berlin 2007.

Ilko-Sascha Kowalczuk, Endspiel. Die Revolution von 1989 in der DDR, Munich 2009.

Ulrich Mählert, Kleine Geschichte der DDR, Munich 2009.

Andreas Malycha/Peter Jochen Winters, Die SED. Geschichte einer deutschen Partei, Munich 2009.

Helmut Müller-Enbergs et al. (Ed.), Wer war wer in der DDR? Ein Lexikon ostdeutscher Biographien, 2 volp., Berlin 2010.

Ehrhart Neubert, Geschichte der Opposition in der DDR 1949–1990, Berlin 1997.

Jens Schöne, Das sozialistische Dorf. Bodenreform und Kollektivierung in der Sowjetzone und DDR, Leipzig 2011.

Klaus Schroeder, Der SED-Staat. Geschichte und Strukturen der DDR 1949–1990, Cologne/Weimar/Vienna 2013.

André Steiner, Von Plan zu Plan. Eine Wirtschaftsgeschichte der DDR, Berlin 2007.

Bernd Stöver, Der Kalte Krieg. Geschichte eines radikalen Zeitalters, Munich 2007.

Stefan Wolle, Die heile Welt der Diktatur. Alltag und Herrschaft in der DDR 1971–1989, Berlin 2013.

LIST OF SOURCES

This book is based on sources from the following archives:

Archives at the Federal Commissioner for the Records of the State Security Service of the former German Democratic Republic (BStU)

Archives at the Federal Foundation for the Reappraisal of the SED Dictatorship
Archives at the Humboldt University of Berlin
The Brandenburg Main State Archive
German Federal Archives
Federal Archives in Berlin
Police Historical Collection Berlin
Robert-Havemann Archive
Saxony State Archives

LIST OF ILLUSTRATIONS

Archives at the Federal Foundation for the Reappraisal of the SED Dictatorship: p. 105 bottom, - Harald Schmitt stock: - Bild Schmitt_420 p. 146, - Bild Schmitt_416 p. 171; - Klaus Mehner stock: - Bild 77_1104_KUL_DDR-Musik_26 p. 169, - Bild 85_0910_POL_Credit_01 p. 187, - Bild 87_0608_KUL-Musik_03 p. 192, - Bild 87_0527_POL_WP-Abruest_12 p. 194, - Bild 89_1024_POL_Demo_04 p. 225 top, - Bild 89_1104_POL-Demo_35 p. 226/227, - Bild 89_1104_POL-Demo_110 p. 228/229, - Bild 89_1109_POL-IPZ_02 p. 233, - Bild 89_1110_POL_DDR-Wende_06 p. 236 bottom, - Bild 89_1110_POL_DDR-Wende_0 p. 237, - Bild 89_1114_POL_VK_9teWP_34 p. 250, - Bild 90_0630_WIF_Konsum_41 p. 266; - Rosemarie Gentges stock: Bild 326 p. 202/203; - Uwe Gerig stock: - Bild 5015 p. 206, - Bild 5093 p. 238/239, - Bild 6319 p. 242/243; - Rainer Eppelmann premortem bequest_Bornholmer_Brücke, photographer Wirth p. 235; **Archiv Bürgerbewegung Leipzig, photographer: Karl-Heinz Müller**: p. 258; **Archiv Verlag**: p. 27, 71, 136, 154, 185; **Axel Springer Verlag INFOPOOL**: p. 137; **Paul Bernharend (photographer; source material: Stiftung Haus der Geschichte, Zeitgeschichtliches Forum Leipzig)**: back cover 2. from top, p. 67; **BStU**: 69, 70 (2), 74 top, 75 middle right, 80/81 top; **Bundesarchiv**: - Plak 100-031-034, Boehner Werbung p. 29, B 145 Bild-D00022155, Georg Munker p. 43,- Bild 183-G1122-0600-130, anon. p. 47, - Bild 183-15410-0009, Heinz Junge p. 59, - Bild 183-24300-0057, Horst Sturm p. 87, - Bild 183-75110-0001, anon. p. 92, - Bild 183-63679-0011, Schmidt p. 134, - Bild 183-K0615-0001-109, anon. p. 144/145, - Bild 183-A1212-0006-001, Irene Eckleben p. 167, - Bild 183-S1104-0002, Ulrich Häßler p. 176, - Bild 183-W0810-0017, Karl-Heinz Schindler p.177, - Bild 183-1990-1003-003, Peer Grimm p. 244, - Bild 183-1990-0304-022, Jan Peter Kasper p. 263, - Bild 183-1990-0831-019, Bernd Settnik p. 269; **FES/AdsD**: p. 48, 68, 72 top, 73 top left, 73 top right, 74 middle, 75 middle left, 80/81 bottom; **Research institute at the German Council on Foreign Relations, 1987**: p. 38 top; **Fanny Heidenreich**: picture of the author; **Berlin Story Museum**: p. 97; **Landesarchiv Berlin**: -/H. von der Becke p. 76/77, -/Peter Cürlis p. 72 bottom, -/Richard Perlia p. 73 bottom left, -/Bert Sass p. 74 bottom, -/Max Schirner p. 75 top, 78/79, -/Gert Schütz p. 73 bottom right, -/Horst Siegmann p. 82, 114 bottom, 115 bottom; **Peter Leibing, Hamburg**: p. 104; **NARA**: p. 39, 105 top, 108 top, 109 (2), 110 bottom, 111 (2), 113 (2), 116 middle, 116 bottom, 117 (2), 118 (2), 119 (3), 125, 129, 240/241; **Photonet.de/ Lehnartz**: p. 106/107; **Police Historical Collection Berlin**: back cover middle, p. 44, 52/53, 73 middle, 75 bottom, 102, 103 (2), 108 bottom, 112, 116 top, 200/201, 247; **picture alliance**: - dpa p. 16, - AP p. 115 top; **Federal Press Office**: B 145 Bild-00048987, Christian Seebode p. 216; **Robert-Havemann-Gesellschaft e.V.**: p. 225 bottom, 251, -/Bernd Albrecht p. 189, -/Nikolaus Becker p. 220, 221, -/ Aram Radomsky p. 199 bottom, -/Siegbert Schefke p. 191, 224 bottom, -/Hanno Schmidt p. 219, -/Rolf Walter p. 253; **Robert-Havemann-Gesellschaft (source)**: Günter Antrack p. 230 bottom, André Böhm p. 231 bottom, BStU-copy back cover 2. from bottom, p. 170, 190, 222, 223, 231 middle, Klaus Dombrowsky p. 273, Sergej Glanze p. 230 top, Jürgen Hohmuth/zeitort.de p. 236 top, Andreas Kämper p. 257, Lutz Mittelbach p. 252, Jürgen Nagel p. 281, Jurino Reetz p. 179, Michael Schroedter/zeitort.de p. 231 top, Matthias Weber p. 273, Rolf Zöllner p. 254, 255, 261, Gerald Zörner p. 272 bottom; **Michael Trippel/laif**: p. 274/275; **ullsteinbild**: p. 37, 89, -/ADN-Bildarchiv p. 133, 199 top, 259, 268, -/Alex Waidmann p. 114 top, -/amw p. 267, -/AP p. 217, -/Bera p. 182, -/Bohuslav p. 139, -/BPA p. 197, -/Danigel p. 248/249, -/ ddrbildarchiv.de/Uhlenhut p. 153 top, -/dpa 26, 172, -/Gircke p. 40, -/Herbert Schulze p. 10, -/Klaus Winkler p. 184, -/Lehnartz p. 120, -/ Müller-Preisser p. 181, -/Ulrich Baumgarten p. 270; **Erik Weiss**: p. 209; **Wikimedia commons** (under the Creative Commons-Lizenz CC-BY-SA 2.5 | https://creativecommons.org/licenses/by-sa/2.5/de/): - TUBS p. 15; **Wikimedia commons** (under the Creative Commons-Lizenz CC-BY-SA 3.0 | https://creativecommons.org/licenses/by-sa/3.0/de/): - anagoria p. 56, - Roehrensee p. 204/205, - Wik1966total p. 215 (2), - NordNordWest p. 269; **Wikimedia commons/German Federal Archives** (under the Creative Commons-Lizenz CC-BY-SA | https://creativecommons.org/licenses/by-sa/3.0/de/): - Bild 183-1982-0413-007, Ulrich Häßler p. 12, - Bild 183-V01850, anon. p. 21, - Bild 183-R67561, anon. p. 25, - Bild 183-32584-0002, Erich Höhne p. 35, - Bild 183-W1126-311, Kolbe Backcover 1. from top, p. 41, - Bild 183-S88792, Eva Kemlein p. 42, - Bild 183-S96390, Günther Paalzow p. 55, - B 145 Bild-F000250-0041, anon. p. 58, - Bild 183-15844-0008, Horst Sturm p. 60, - Bild 183-16892-0005, Illner p. 61, - Bild 183-24320-0002, Heinz-Günter Quaschinski p. 62, - Bild 183-16144-0006, Krueger p. 63 bottom, - Bild 183-18666-0033, Klein p. 65, - Bild 183-40377-0007, Wittig p. 91, - Bild 183-52061-0023, Schmidt p. 94, - Bild 183-57000-0139, anon. p. 95, - Bild 183-83911-0002, anon. p. 101, - Bild 183-85458-0001, Heinz Junge p. 110 top, - Bild 183-C0304-0091-020, Peter Heinz Junge p. 131, - Bild 183-B0115-0010-027, anon. p. 135, - Bild 183-F0418-0001-038, Ulrich Kohls p. 141, - Bild 183-11076-0006, Seidel p. 142, - Bild 183-K0614-0006-003, Wolfgang Thieme p. 143, - Bild 183-G0301-0001-009, Friedrich Gahlbeck p. 150 top, - Bild 183-M0611-0007, Sigrid Kutscher (married Kubiziel) p. 150 bottom, - Bild 183-K0507-0004-001, Hubert Link p. 151 top, - Bild 183-N0621-0017, anon. p. 151 bottom, - Bild 183-T0519-0006, Erwin Schneider p. 152 top, - Bild 183-Z0318-032, Hubert Link p. 152 bottom, - Bild 183-N0331-0028, Joachim Spremberg p. 153 bottom, - Bild 183-U0328-0029, Hartmut Reiche p. 155, - Bild 183-J0814-0008-001, Waltraud Raphael (married Grubitzsch) p. 157, - Bild 183-N0622-0035, Rainer Mittelstädt p. 158, - Bild 183-P1017-0317, Rainer Mittelstädt p. 169, - Bild 183-P0801-026, Horst Sturm p. 160, - Bild 183-R0423-0026, Peter Heinz Junge p. 163, - Bild 183-R1001-0048, Hubert Link p. 164, - Bild 183-1987-0907-13, Rainer Mittelstädt p. 195, - Bild 183-1990-0922-002, Friedrich Gahlbeck p. 224 top, - Bild 183-1989-1109-030, Thomas Lehmann p. 234, - Bild 183-1990-0210-001, Gabriele Senft p. 264; - Bild 183-1990-1003-036, Bernd Settnik p. 272 top; **Wikimedia commons/Deutsche Fotothek**: p. 31, 66; **Wikimedia commons/public domain**: p. 7, 20, 22, 33, 38 bottom, 45, 63 top, 90, 100, 161, 185 (2); **Siegfried Wittenburg**: p. 183

ACKNOWLEDGMENT

The journey is over. Over the past seven years, I have had the pleasure of being able to write numerous books about various aspects of GDR's history. The book you are holding was the next logical step. In this respect, I would firstly like to thank the Berlin Story Verlag for giving me this opportunity. In particular, I would like to give my sincere thanks to Stephanie Hönicke, Norman Bösch and Wieland Giebel.

I would also like to thank staff in the archives and libraries. Likewise, I would like to thank all the contemporary witnesses who agreed to to talk to me about fine details, as well as the bigger picture. Thank you for a few eye-opening (and often amusing) hours. Dr. Jenni Englert read the manuscript with great attention to detail and improved it noticeably. Furthermore, I thank all my colleagues with whom I have had many helpful conversations and who commented on parts of my work or helped me with specific questions. For support and inspiration of different kinds, I would like to thank: Dr. Bärbel Fest, Sylvia Griwan, Fanny Heidenreich, the Monsters and Christoph Wunnicke.

This book is dedicated to my family, Conrad in particular.

BERLIN STORY

Unter den Linden
Brandenburger Tor

Anhalter Bahnhof
Mendelssohn-Bartholdy-Park